My Daily Life Coach

Volume 1
Calling

Clarifying the Nature of Your Assignment

Anthony L. Stringer

CREATING A LEGACY OF INSPIRATION

ALLRIZE MEDIA

Your word is a lamp to my feet

and a light to my path.

Psalm 119:105 NKJV

My Daily Life Coach
Volume 1 - Calling by Anthony Stringer

Copyright © 2024 by Anthony Stringer

First printing February 2024

ISBN: 979-8-9873442-4-8

Cover Design by Allrize Media

Printed in the United States of America

ALLRIZE MEDIA

www.allrizemedia.com

In their hearts humans plan their course,

but the Lord establishes their steps.

Proverbs 16:9 NIV

Table of Contents

Introduction to My Daily Life Coach - *Can Your Hear the Whistle* — 1

Introduction to Volume One: Calling - *A Place for Every Piece* — 7

Chapter 1 - Light Your Path - *The Milestone of Bible Study* — 12

Chapter 2 - Accept the Invitation - *The Milestone of Communion* — 22

Chapter 3 - Speak Life - *The Milestone of Declaration* — 30

Chapter 4 - Change Your Target - *The Milestone of Discernment* — 38

Chapter 5 - Let Your Crack Show - *The Milestone of Evangelism* — 46

Chapter 6 - Raise Your Expectations - *The Milestone of Expectation* — 54

Chapter 7 - Break the Cycle - *The Milestone of Freedom* — 62

Chapter 8 - Reach Beyond Your Now - *The Milestone of Hope* — 70

Chapter 9 - Fix the Flat - *The Milestone of Inspiration* — 78

Chapter 10 - Keep Asking Questions - *The Milestone of Investigation* — 86

Table of Contents

Chapter 11 - Talk to Your Friend - *The Milestone of Prayer*   94

Chapter 12 - Speak Truth to Power - *The Milestone of Prophecy*   102

Chapter 13 - Live on Purpose - *The Milestone of Purpose*   110

Chapter 14 - Make the Most of It - *The Milestone of Stewardship*   118

Chapter 15 - Dance in the Rain - *The Milestone of Submission*   126

Chapter 16 - Assume the Position - *The Milestone of Victory*   134

Chapter 17 - Change Your Arsenal - *The Milestone of Warfare*   142

References

Introduction To My Daily Life Coach
"Can You Hear the Whistle"

A coach is a visionary who sees the champion in you that you may not readily see in yourself. Consequently, it brings the coach no greater joy than for you to reach a level of skill, proficiency, and competence that you never imagined would be possible. However, shifting from where you are now to where you can ultimately become is an uphill journey that requires commitment and determination. Not in the form of flawless perfection, but rather through the lessons learned from enduring the pain of your mistakes, taking accountability for your actions, and rising from the ashes of your defeats.

The words of your success story will be written from the scars of your journey. What have you learned from the things that you have endured? How have they influenced your decisions going forward? What do they teach you about yourself? What do they teach you about your God?

In his final words to the Disciples, Jesus said, "I will send you another Comforter[1]" The purpose of this comforter is not to make you comfortable, but rather to serve as your Daily Life Coach. Like Jesus, perhaps the Comforter may descend upon you in the peacefulness of a dove[2] However, He comes to reside in you with the intensity of a coach.

He blows the whistle whenever you introduce a foul on the field of your purpose. He blows the whistle whenever you step outside of the boundary lines established in His word.

1

He then blows the whistle between quarters when your rest and recovery is in order. He is the lifter of your head, the fire in your belly, and the wind beneath your wings.

It is wasteful to pour a gallon of water into an eight-ounce glass, because the capacity of the glass is limited. Such is the case with your life as a believer. Throughout your walk with the Lord, your capacity is intended to be in a constant state of expansion. Your condition does not have to be your conclusion. God always has more of Himself to reveal to you, more of His power to release through you, and more of His blessing to bestow upon you. However, He can only pour into you what you can handle. Wanting more is not the same as being able to handle more.

As your daily life coach, His role is to provide wisdom and insight that will facilitate your holistic growth and development. It is His job to stir the pot of your potential so that the power within you can be released into the atmosphere around you. It is His job to remind you who you are, and the standard to which you are called. It is His job to challenge you to engage in a deep-sea dive into the depths of your character to identify and to discard the weights that hinder your intended impact.

As your soul yearns for a more meaningful connection to God, you may often recognize that there are significant gaps that threaten this connection. However, it is not always readily apparent what these gaps are, or what an effective approach to close them may look like. A milestone is an action or event marking a significant change or stage in development.

My Daily Life Coach was written to bring to the forefront of your consciousness fifty (50) growth and development milestones across three book volumes, in hopes that the Comforter will reveal areas in your heart that may require recalibration. Consequently, this book was written for anyone who desires a closer walk with the Lord. Whether you are at the beginning of your journey, or if you are a seasoned believer, there is great value to be discovered, reinforced, and revisited throughout the pages of this book and the other two (2) volumes pertaining to the nature of the calling God has for your life.

Layout, Content, and Style

There are three (3) volumes to this book. In this book, Volume one (1) *Clarifying the Nature of Your Assignment*, you are invited to engage in a devotional overview of seventeen (17) significant milestones that contribute to personal growth and development. Central themes throughout this book include: aligning with God's direction for your life, personal engagement in the process of your growth, impacting your sphere of influence, regulating your priorities, and discerning between good pursuits and God pursuits. Each milestone is comprised of eleven (11) key components: Title, Scripture, Focal Point, Overview, Prayer Target, Meaning, Calling, Challenges, Process, Results, and Mirror Moments.

Title
The titles of each milestone entry are intentionally action-oriented (keep, check, accept, avoid, build, fix, wait, etc.) to emphasize the need for your personal engagement in your calling.

Scripture
There is a key scripture provided, as well as additional scriptures at various points throughout the milestone discussion. Several of these will have a superscripted number that can be referenced in the associated section at the back of the book (i.e. Comforter [3]). Unless otherwise specified, all scriptures are based on the King James Version (KJV) of the Bible.

Focal Point
This is a statement that is pulled from the overview that you can meditate on throughout your day and serves as an anchor for the milestone under consideration.

Overview
An effort is made at the outset of every milestone, to provide relevant information in relatable language and common scenarios (i.e. restless toddler, hot beverage, etc.), or contemporary examples (i.e. Queen of England, etc.), to draw a parallel to the meaning of the milestone that is being presented.

Prayer Target
This is a short statement of prayer to offer you a good starting point in approaching the Lord for growth in the milestone under consideration.

Meaning
This milestone component offers an opportunity to dig beneath the face-value of the milestone and gain further understanding of its characteristics. This offers a standard against which your life can be examined. What does it mean to have discernment, to be compassionate, to be a good steward, or to be a peacemaker?

Calling

This milestone component seeks to show you the relevance of this milestone to your life; that this extends beyond being a "nice-to-have" area of character development, to a scriptural expectation that God has placed on your life. Is this really something that God requires of me? How can I be so sure? What is the standard against which I can examine my life?

Challenges

This milestone component considers potential obstacles, whether within or without, that you can expect to encounter as you seek to answer the call for development in this area. What thoughts and perspectives need to change? What behaviors do I need to be aware of and keep in check?

Process

This milestone component provides practical steps that you can readily implement to experience growth in that respective area. Who do I need to connect with to support my commitment to grow? What short and long term goals do I need to write down and rehearse regularly?

Results

This milestone component provides insight into the expected outcome of allowing growth and development to occur in your life. What will it mean for me? What will it mean for those in my sphere of influence, my marriage, my children, and my community?

Mirror Moments

These questions are provided for you to consider where you currently stand in relation to the expectations of the milestone being considered. They are not intended to be indictments of your weaknesses, but rather personal reflections that can serve to fuel ongoing character development.

Application

Each of the milestones and their respective components are not exhaustive in nature but are rather designed to serve as a catalyst for further investigation and conversation. The layout is structured in a manner that lends itself well as the basis for an outline that can be used for personal bible study, life group topics and fuel for discussion, and workshop or sermon preparation. Each of the milestones can also be approached as a weekly study, where one of the milestone components of meaning, calling, challenges, process, and results, can be examined and focused on each day of the week from Monday through Friday.

Regardless of your chosen approach to considering the milestones presented in this book, it is my prayer that you will find valuable tools and insight that will enable ongoing growth and development. It is my prayer that you will experience life in all the fullness and abundance intended for all believers. It is my prayer that you will approach each milestone with an open and honest heart, committed to remain on the potter's wheel until the Lord, the Comforter, the Divine *Daily Life Coach* fashions you into an image that is reflective of His own. Let the journey begin.

Introduction To Volume One - Calling
"A Place for Every Piece"

It is one of the greatest joys of parenthood to see your children relate to the world around them as they grow and develop beyond infancy. It is almost as though with each child, you yourself are reborn and reintroduced to the intricate shapes, rich colors, myriad of sounds, and array of smells that are so often taken for granted in the world around you. Critical to this journey is an essential childhood developmental milestone, commonly referred to as "Fine Motor Skills." This refers to the coordination of the muscles with the eyes, hands, and the fingers to accomplish a task.

A classic example of a tool used both to demonstrate and evaluate fine motor skills, is a puzzle consisting of shapes such as circles, squares, rectangles, and triangles. The object is for the child to match the shape with its appropriate opening in the puzzle. It is interesting to watch the frustration that the child displays when trying to fit the square in the round opening or the triangle in the star-shaped opening. The goal is understood. The resources are provided to accomplish the goal. Yet the goal cannot be accomplished based on the terms set by the child. The terms have already been set, and it is left to the child to recognize those terms to accomplish the goal.

Have you ever felt the frustration of the child, or the pain of the shape, being screamed at and pounded on to fit into or conform to something that you knew wasn't right for you? Perhaps you have witnessed the chaos and competition that ensues amongst those trying to fit into places for which their skill set was never designed.

No one has been given the license to set the terms wherein their gifts, skills, talent, and experience is to be utilized. There is a unique calling or assignment for which you were created and if you find yourself struggling to identify what it is, know that the kingdom of God is calling all castaways; those who don't fit in, measure up, or make the cut of what is acceptable to the status quo of this world.

Notice, in calling you, God did not lower the standard. Rather, He functions according to an entirely different standard; a higher one; the criteria of which does not regard any wisdom, strength, or pedigree that does not originate in, or flow from God. Yes, you have been hand-picked by God. Yes, you with all the historical baggage that is attached to you; the stuff you tried to hide in the closet, sweep under the rug, or bury deep in the woods of regret. Nothing that you have thought, said, or done has disqualified you from the assignment God has for your life.

Yes, there are actions you can take and choices you can make that can regretfully surprise you. And yes, God may be hurt or disappointed by your actions. However, He is never surprised. He is never caught off guard. He doesn't hold grudges. And He has already established a way for you to get back on the right track. Don't allow yourself to get lost in the dark cave of doubting your value and worthiness. The most important thing to keep in mind is that your worthiness is never self-imposed. It is God who counts you worthy of the assignment by laying his worthiness on you like a robe. It is not merit-based. It is a gift that cannot be earned, only received.

Regularly announce to the voices of guilt and shame in your life, that you are worthy, because God makes you worthy. You have what it takes regardless of your ability. You are qualified not based on your ability, but your availability. When was the last time you said yes Lord? Yes, to your will for my life. Yes, to your assignment on my life.

Whether you realize it or not, greatness lies inside of you. It is not your greatness. It is the greatness of God that has been placed there to impact those in your sphere of influence. No, the greatness does not belong to you. However, you are the steward of that greatness. You are responsible for managing that greatness in a manner that honors God. This means that you will be held accountable for what He has deposited in you. This is not meant as a threat to stir up doubt and anxiety. Rather it should serve as the hope that fuels the passion and drive that you invest in your calling; to hear Him say, "Well done thy good and faithful servant.[1]" It is this hope that should be used to sharpen your focus and embolden you to silence the voices of your distractions.

Yes, it requires a heightened level of intentionality to manage pleasures that conflict with your calling. It is for this reason that we hear Paul saying, "I press toward the mark.[2]" Pressing suggests that doing so is not the natural inclination of the heart, as there would be no need to press against something if it were not in turn pressing against you. So, pressing calls for a sense of dedicated intentionality to carry out the assignment God has for your life, realizing that nothing is more important than the "high calling" to which you have been called.

In addition, it is a "holy calling.[3]" This means it is unparalleled to anything in this world. God is holy. To understand the holiness of God is to recognize that it is the sum of His multifaceted nature, his love, his mercy, his judgment, etc.[4] All these aspects are in perfect proportion in God and are what gives Him the distinction of being holy. Being the recipient of a holy calling, means that a measure of all of who God is, has been deposited in what He has called you to do. In fact, the expectation is not that you would just "do the work" of your calling, but rather that you would "optimize the work" of your calling. You are called to great demonstration and impact in your sphere of influence. Your calling is not an afterthought in the mind of God. He saw you operating in and optimizing it before the foundation of the world.

So, as you investigate the aspects of this great calling to which you have been called in the following pages, do so in full assurance that your yes is the key to your success. Your yes to God is more powerful than any no that would oppose you. Your yes and the actions that demonstrate it are the greatest expression of your faith that the same God who began the great work in you will continue it until the day of Jesus Christ.[5]

Light Your Path
The Milestone of Bible Study

The entrance of thy words giveth light; it giveth understanding unto the simple.
Psalm 119:30

God's word will always lead you to where God is.
My Daily Life Coach

Imagine, being in the middle of a storm, the strength of which was so powerful, that it took away the light in your house. It's nighttime. Can you hear the rain pounding on your roof? Do you hear the eerily loud and boisterous claps of thunder? Can you see intermittent flashes of lighting without warning?

The wind continues to howl, knocking down trees, and blowing all manner of debris toward and around your house. As if this scene is not unsettling enough, you are forced to wait out the storm in the darkness of your home. To move to a more secure place, you carefully navigate, feeling with your hands. Yet, you find yourself bumping into and stumbling over furniture in your path.

What you wouldn't do, to have a flashlight or a candle; something to pierce through the darkness and help you to get to a place of safety and comfort. The desperation of this scene is like that being expressed in the context of the opening passage.

Apart from God, your world is in utter darkness. Despite your efforts, you are stumbling around, trying to make sense of the unsensible, embracing the lies of fulfillment, chasing the winds of your fantasies, and drinking the vanity of pride and self-sufficiency. As a believer, you are expected to walk by faith and not by sight.[1] The only way you can receive faith is through the word of the Lord.[2] It is through the light of God's word that you can navigate through the darkness of this world. God's word will always lead you to where God is. This is your place of safety and security. This is your hiding place. This is your refuge[3] amid the storms of life.

Lord, help me live my life in the light
of your word.

Bible Study - The Meaning

Bible Study is the life-long practice of searching the scriptures for information concerning the past, present, and future realities of God's presence and purpose for his people. The words of the Bible hold an authority that exceeds the authority from any other source. Its words are true for all time and for all people .

So why should you study the Bible? It equips you to live the way God wants you to live. The teachings of the Bible help you to learn the truth about God, yourself, and the world around you. When its truths are applied to your life, it changes wrong ways of thinking and acting. The Bible also provides you with the training to adopt righteous living principles and it gives you examples of the rewards experienced by those who applied these principles to their lives.

Mirror Moment
What are some righteous living principles that are taught in the word of God?

Bible Study - The Calling

Study to shew thyself approved unto God, a workman that needeth not to be ashamed, rightly dividing the word of truth.

II Timothy 2:15

The calling of Bible Study is to live in the favor and approval of God. You can only give God what He wants, to the extent that you know what that is. Your study of God's word cultivates your heart to produce fruit that brings glory to God. The calling of Bible Study is to live a life free from the bondage of fear and shame. It reveals the truth of who you are and who you belong to. Your identity in God is your greatest superpower. When you know who you are, and what you are capable of through the power of God, nothing can stop what God desires to do through you; the lives you will touch, the impact you will make, and the legacy you will leave.

Mirror Moment

How does knowing that God's word helps me to live above fear and shame affect how I approach it?

Bible Study - The Challenges

There are several challenges that many face when studying the Bible. One of these challenges is that it was written thousands of years ago by people in a much different culture than that of today. What does a book that was written so long ago have to do with my present situation? The simple answer to this question is that the Bible is unlike any other book ever written; it is the word of God, the God of eternity. So just as God is timeless, the truths to be found in His word are timeless truths, relevant to all people, in all places, throughout all generations. When applied to your life, it causes you to experience a fullness of life unmatched by any other source.

Another challenge encountered in Bible study is found in the fact that the Bible contains different types of writing such as poetry, letters, and history. The multi-dimensional design of the Bible is representative of the multi-dimensional God who inspired its every word. Don't miss out on the opportunity to experience the fullness to be had in relationship with God by getting hung up on one aspect of God that you may not agree with. The thing to keep in mind is that God has a reason for everything that he does and everything that he allows, whether we agree with or understand it in the moment.

Perhaps one of the greatest struggles encountered in Bible study is the numerous versions of the Bible that are available today. How do I know which one is the right one? Many have found the original King James Version Bible difficult to understand because of the language that it uses in delivering its message.

To make the message a little easier to understand, different versions of the same Bible have been produced such as the NIV, the Message, and the Voice translations along with many others. The intent of these Bible versions is not to take away from the original meaning but to provide you with further clarity concerning what you are studying.

Mirror Moment

Do I believe that the Bible is relevant to my life and, if so, how do my actions reflect this belief?

Bible Study - The Process

But his delight is in the law of the Lord; and in his law doth he meditate day and night.

Psalm 1:2

So how should you study the Bible? You should study regularly[4] Bible study is a spiritual discipline and as such, it is something that should be adopted into the regular routine of your life. You should also study the Bible systematically. Instead of reading wherever the Bible falls open, find a method that works best for you such as a devotional reading guide that gives daily scriptures for you to consider, followed by a short explanation of the scripture, and a way for you to apply the scripture in your life.

In addition to studying the Bible regularly, you may try studying it creatively. In other words, you may want to use different approaches each time you study. One day, you might read an entire book. The next day you might read a chapter or a shorter portion of scripture. Still another time you may want to study a word, or a theme used throughout the Bible. For instance, you may want to consider what the Bible has to say about love, or forgiveness, or success, or marriage. Still another approach to Bible study may be to study the life of a man or a woman in the Bible such as David, Job, Ruth or Jesus.

Whichever method you choose for Bible study, remember to read with an open mind. Ask yourself questions about what you are reading. This process should be accompanied with prayer asking God to guide you down the path of truth and help you to hear His voice for your situation through the scripture you are reading. What commands am I to follow?

What promises can I embrace? What examples should I follow? What are the sins for which I should repent? What is God requiring of me in this season?

Mirror Moment

What is the most effective method that I have found for me to study the Bible?

Bible Study - The Results

Through the Bible, you are made aware of so many promises that are yours to be enjoyed when in relationship with the Lord such as; "I will never leave you, nor forsake you," or "All things work together for good to them that love God, to them who are the called according to His purpose," or "I know the plans that I think toward you says the Lord, plans to prosper you and to give you a hope and a future."

Studying the Bible sets your expectation that God will deliver on every promise that He has made. Living according to its wisdom causes you to experience its power in your life. To release the benefits of the word into our lives, we must study the word with an obedient spirit. Its truths were not written simply to inform you, but rather for you to take this information and apply it to your life so that you can be fruitful in all that you put your hands to do.

Mirror Moment
Do my decisions tend to be based on the wisdom of man or the wisdom of scripture?

Accept the Invitation
The Milestone of Communion

He brought me to the banqueting house, and his banner over me was love.   *Song of Solomon 2:4*

Don't get comfortable in your current place of blessing or in yesterday's revelation of who God is.

My Daily Life Coach

Have you ever taken the time to really consider how much God loves you? His is a love that doesn't give up easy. Even when rejected, abused, and misused, His love still chases you. Not only is it a love that corrects and rebukes, but it is a love that heals and restores. It is a love that finds you in the forgotten place, even at the bottom of the barrel of your own foolish and misguided choices. It reaches you there and pulls you out. Love washes the filth, clothes you in righteousness, and brings you into the place of blessing.

As we consider the opening scripture, it ought to stir our souls as it along with the entire book of Song of Solomon, provides a portrait of God's relentless love for His people.

22

Notice that it mentions that He brought you into His banqueting house. This means that He had to first find you where you were; involved in whatever you were involved in. Contrary to others in your life, His purpose was not to condemn you; it was to invite you to a celebration that He had prepared in your honor; a celebration of His love for you.

You say, "I have nothing to wear for such an occasion." To which He replies, "I have garments that not only will fit, but have been tailor made with you in mind." You say, "this celebration of your love for me is not a place that I deserve to be." To which He replies, "Your worth to me surpasses anything you have done or left undone; your value exceeds your offence." There isn't an excuse, that you could ever provide that would affect the magnitude of God's love for you, and His desire for you to experience His love at a higher level, and in a better place than you are currently.

God is not boring. God is multifaceted and since God is love, it follows that the love He has for you is a multifaceted love. Don't get comfortable in your current place of blessing or in yesterday's revelation of who God is. Regardless of what you have experienced to this point, there is another level, another place, another banqueting house that he has prepared and into which He desires to bring you. There is no more extravagant love than God's love for you.

Lord, help me to always embrace your invitation to experience your love for me.

23

Communion - The Meaning

Communion is a time when an assembly of believers gather and partake of bread and wine in remembrance of the sacrifice of Christ's body and blood on behalf of our sins; granting the rights of relationship to all who believe in Him. Yet communion with God is not limited to the collective body of believers. Rather, it is also intended to occur regularly on an individual level, where you set aside time to consider God's relentless love for you and to express your love for Him in return.

As significant as Calvary was, it is not the climax of Christ's love for you. It served chiefly as the door through which you can step into a relationship with Him. His desire is for you to experience a multi-dimensional, ever-unfolding love that will be revealed throughout all eternity.[1]

Mirror Moment

How am I addressing the things in my life that compete with my communion with the Lord?

Communion - The Calling

Behold, I stand at the door, and knock: if any man hear my voice, and open the door, I will come in to him, and will sup with him, and he with me.   *Revelation 3:20*

The Bible is God's personal love letter to you. His central message is, "I want you. You have a value to me that is much greater than all of your past offences." Your ability to comprehend what it really means to value and cherish someone begins with answering the calling of God into communion.

It is a humbling reality to see the infinite God of the universe waiting patiently at the doorstep of your heart. Knowing that you could not come to where He is, He came to where you are, because spending uninterrupted, quality time with you is that important to Him. In doing so, He has made communion very simple. All you need to do is open the door.

Mirror Moment
What are the doors in my heart that I struggle to give God access to, even when He already knows what's behind them?

Communion - The Challenges

The central challenge to communion is prioritization. You cannot spend quality time in the presence of the Lord and not be changed for the better in the process. However, you cannot obtain this outcome without making the necessary investment.

One of the most central questions of life is, "How am I spending my time?" The answer to this question will reveal where your priorities lie. Investment implies sacrifice; it is the willingness to make a directional release of something valuable, believing that what I will receive will exceed what I have chosen to release. Time is your most prized possession and amid everything that fights for it, you ultimately decide who wins. Robbing God of His time with you causes you and everyone connected to you to lose. Make quality time for God today.

Mirror Moment
Am I more likely to release my time to God or to redirect my time from God to matters of less importance?

Communion - The Process

The process of communion begins with a decision to open the door upon which God is knocking. Any delay can be detrimental. He comes to where you are, because he has a word for you that is critical for your current season. Any delay only keeps you from making a step that could set the course for the rest of your life.

Don't try to clean up your house before opening the door. He knows the condition of your house and He came anyway because He's after your heart. If He can change the condition of your heart, the condition of your house will follow.

Remember that communion with God is most effective when He does most of the talking. Yes, feel free to share your heart and to honor and praise Him, but be sure that most of the time is spent sitting, standing, kneeling, and or laying in his presence. His silence is golden. Be assured that He is working something wonderful in you even when He is not speaking to you.

Mirror Moment
How do I feel about spending time with the Lord even when I cannot hear his voice or feel His presence?

Communion - The Results

There is no better way of understanding your value to God than by spending quality time in his presence. So many voices seek to challenge the significance of your efforts and your self-esteem. These voices come from within as well as without. There is nothing more fulfilling and empowering than having the Lord tell you how much you mean to Him.

Communion is a critical key to humility. The more time you spend with the Lord, the more He reveals himself to you. The more you see of God, the less you see of yourself as you come to realize that He alone is the center of attraction of the entire universe throughout all eternity.

Mirror Moment
How much different would my life be if I became less focused on what I am not receiving, and more focused on giving God what He requires from me?

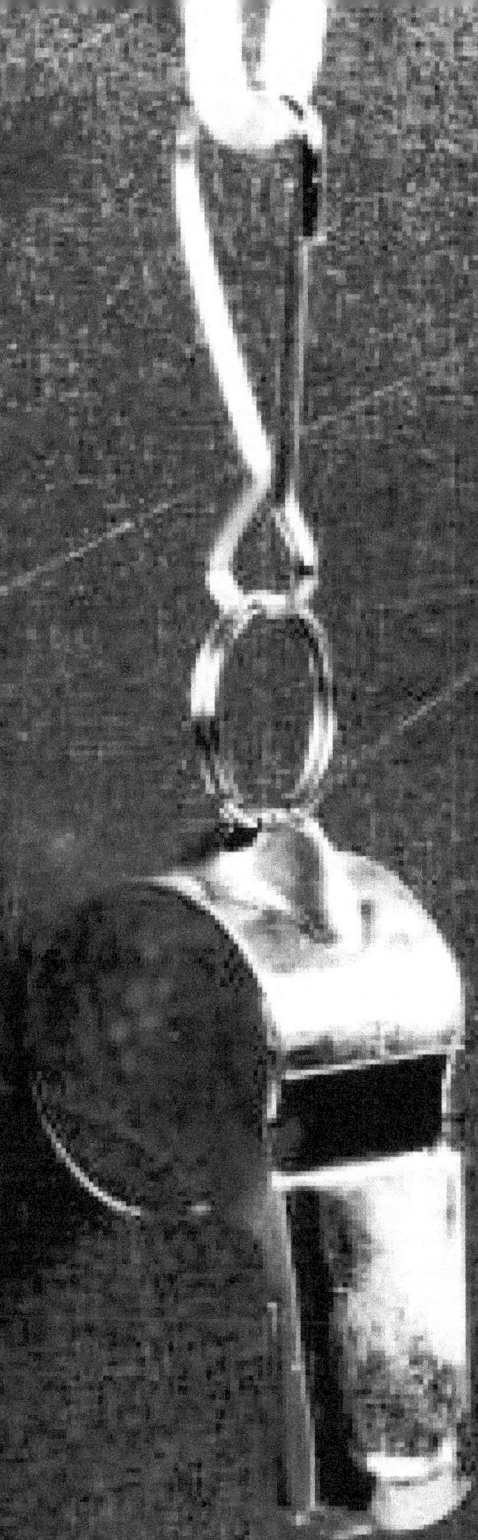

Speak Life
The Milestone of Declaration

I shall not die, but live, and declare the works of the Lord.

Psalm 118:17

...the same God that lit the fire in you, also created the water that your enemies are using in their vain attempts to extinguish your flame.

My Daily Life Coach

Have you ever known, read, or heard of anyone who survived a near death experience? Perhaps they were in a horrible car accident. Maybe it was an unfavorable prognosis from the doctor; a heart or blood condition from which it seemed impossible for them to recover. However, somehow against all odds, the bed of sickness transformed into a bed of recovery from which the person rose beyond any recognition of their previous predicament.

Such phenomenal occurrences are clearly understood by recognizing that God alone sets our time of departure. His will overrides even our foolish choices to gamble with the vapor of our own lives. Only the God who starts your fire can extinguish it.

It is not by mistake that the birth of the New Testament church involved the appearance of fire.[1] When you were born again, God lit a fire in you. Like the author in the opening passage, you too, can take comfort in the fact that the same God that lit your fire also created the water with which your enemies desire to extinguish your flame. Don't be afraid of the threats of the enemy because that's all that they are: empty threats. They have no teeth and no claws. They may touch you. They may touch your family. They may challenge your faith. However, they can never extinguish your flame.

As in the opening passage, rehearse this truth to yourself and make it known to those in your circle of acquaintance. Tell of the works of the Lord. Brag on God. Fill your atmosphere with praise and worship to the God who preserves and prevails.

Lord, give me the boldness to declare your word in every season of my life.

Declaration - The Meaning

At any given point when two teams compete, one is considered as being on the defensive side, and the other is on the offensive side. The team, trying to score, is considered as being on the offensive.

Declaration is the act of speaking from an offensive position. It is your move, and you are called upon to set the tone in each situation, by speaking victory or defeat over yourself or others in your sphere of influence. There is a direct relationship between the weight of your declaration[2] and the level of your authority. The declaration of a king is vastly more significant than the declaration of a soldier unless the soldier is speaking on behalf of the king.

Nothing can stand in the way of a child of God who declares the word of God according to the will of God. Stop speaking from a defensive, defeated position. Remember you speak on behalf of the king. The change you desire to see in your life is waiting on your declaration.

Mirror Moment
Am I declaring what God has to say concerning what I am facing?

Declaration - The Calling

Declare his glory among the heathen, his wonders among all people.

Psalms 96:3

The calling of declaration is to share the revelation of who God is with those who are unaware of it. The awesomeness of your experience with God is not for your benefit and blessing only.

Daily, you are confronted with people who have no idea that their life can be any different than it currently is; that they do not have to be bound to the circumstances of their lives; and to what is dictated to them by those in power. When you declare "Thy kingdom come,[3]" you are declaring that God's kingdom will come alive even in the lives of those who are oblivious to it.

Don't believe the lies of the enemy that your experience with God is to be limited to private contemplation. Or that there is a universal spirit of rejection among those who have yet to experience God for themselves. Without God there is only existence; there is no life. Just as God breathed into Adam the breath of life,[4] through your declaration, you too are called to breathe life into your sphere of influence.

Mirror Moment
How am I speaking life into my surroundings regardless how they appear?

Declaration - The Challenges

One of the major challenges facing your declarations of faith, is finding peace in the gap between what you declare and what you see. Remember, Noah continued the construction of the ark for 70+ years before the rain came[5]. The only thing that he had was the only thing that he needed which was a word from the Lord.

It was an insane concept at the time to think of water falling from the sky. Can you imagine what those around him were thinking or saying? Yet, just as the heavens declare God's works[6], Noah's work declared the superiority of the word of God to any other voice he may have encountered. It is for this reason that it is not enough to hear what God said. You must declare what He has said and keep it on repeat in your heart despite the circumstances around you that may contradict it.

Mirror Moment

What declarations have I backed away from because I didn't see the results that I expected to see?

Declaration - The Process

And he said unto them, this kind can come forth by nothing, but by
prayer and fasting. *Mark 9:29*

You cannot declare a word that you have not received. Receiving is not the same as hearing. Your receiving of God's word is demonstrated by what you do with it. Do you put it on the shelf, or do you rest it on the throne of your heart?

Declaring is more than repeating. Remember for your declaration to have its intended impact, it must be spoken from a place of authority. Your relationship with Christ establishes your place of authority, yet you must make the necessary investments into your relationship with Him in order to see the full impact of the authority that you possess.

In the above passage the disciples could not bring about healing in a certain situation in scripture. When Jesus provided the healing, he emphasized to the disciples the significance of prayer and fasting. He showed through demonstration the direct relationship between consecration and authority. The power of God comes through consistent time in His transformative presence. This is what causes your declarations to move the mountains that stand in your way.[7]

Mirror Moment
What steps can I take to increase the excercise of my spiritual
authority?

Declaration - The Results

By consistently declaring the word of the Lord, you set the tone for your life; a winning tone that victoriously faces any obstacle that you will encounter. It reminds you of who you are and what you do not have to accept.

By declaring the word of the Lord, you not only bring the kingdom of heaven to earth, but you also make it alive and active in your life and the lives of others. Your declaration is fundamental to any change that you desire to see. Just as God observed the emptiness and formlessness of the earth and said let there be, remember the same transformative word resides in you.

Mirror Moment
Do I tend to conform to my circumstances as they are, or am I using my words to transform them into what they can become?

Change Your Target
The Milestone of Discernment

For we wrestle not against flesh and blood, but against principalities, against powers, against the rulers of the darkness of this world, against spiritual wickedness in high places.

Ephesians 6:12

The enemy will use anyone to whom he has access, as a human shield, to impair the progress of God's purpose in your life.

My Daily Life Coach

If you have ever seen the news or watched a documentary on crime, you have likely come across the term plea bargain. In this arrangement, the defendant agrees to plead guilty to a particular charge in return for a concession from the prosecutor. A case and point may involve an individual who is arrested and charged with drug possession.

Knowing that the real threat to the drug problem is bigger than this one individual, the authorities may be motivated to strike a plea bargain. If they can use this person to find the source of the drugs, that would go further in removing them from the street.

Paul is informing us to utilize this same approach in the spiritual realm, where our focus should be to defeat the real threat. Making this distinction of targets requires discernment. The enemy will use anyone to whom he has access, as a human shield, to impair the progress of God's purpose in your life. Seeing the person as the threat causes you to waste your time attacking the wrong target.

Is it an unreasonable or belligerent supervisor that you see every day? Is it someone that you consider a dear friend? Perhaps it is someone in your house; a child or a spouse? Though the shield is what you can see, the real enemy is hiding behind the shield.

Remember that the shield is not the enemy. Instead, the shield is what the enemy uses to protect itself when attacking you. Distinguishing between the shield and the enemy, requires discernment. How do you gain the victory over the one using the shield? The only way is through the word. The Word of God is so powerful that it can impair the real enemy and preserve the person that the enemy is using, at the same time.

Lord, help me to recognize the real enemy and to defeat him through your word.

Discernment - The Meaning

Discernment is the spiritual resource that sees more than what meets the eye. Like an x-ray machine, discernment allows you to see the reality of the brokenness and misalignment beneath the surface of a person or a situation. Discernment also serves as the antenna for the believer that senses when God is moving and distinguishes His voice amid the noise of your surroundings.

Mirror Moment

Do I impulsively respond to people based on their actions, or do I allow time to understand where their present behavior is coming from?

Discernment - The Calling

*Prove all things; hold fast that which is good. Abstain from all
appearance of evil.* *I Thessalonians 5:21-22*

Discernment is the calling to live a filtered life, where you are ever
mindful of the ideas you embrace and the activities in which you
engage. It is the calling to recognize and gravitate toward God's
expectation for your life at all costs. What God values should be
what you value. Likewise, you should be found standing in sharp
opposition to anything that God opposes. Discernment is the
calling to be uncompromising in your identity; unafraid to draw
the line across which you refuse to allow anything that displeases
God.

Mirror Moment
*Do I see the value in filtering the things that I watch or listen to, and
do my actions reflect this value?*

Discernment - The Challenges

For that which I do I allow not: for what I would, that do I not; but what I hate, that do I.   *Romans 7:15*

A central challenge to growing in discernment is the self-discipline that it requires. Sustaining a posture of Godly engagement requires living against the grain of your comfort and convenience. Hearing God clearly and sensing when He is at work, requires you to be tuned into Him. This means that the guard at the gate to your heart cannot be allowed to clock out, take a break, fall asleep, or go on vacation.

This guard is your self-discipline which seeks to convince you that your efforts to remain faithful are excessive and unnecessary; that you are kidding yourself to think that this time will be any different than your past attempts. Faithfulness is not the same as flawlessness. God sees and honors your every attempt to remain faithful in the face of your weaknesses and failures.

Mirror Moment
What excuses am I making to explain why I am not more self-disciplined, and how long will I allow myself to be ruled by them?

Discernment - The Process

As it relates to growing in discernment there is no substitute for a lifestyle of consecration. Seeing your world clearly through God's eyes is achieved only through dedicated times of giving Him your undivided attention by putting personal pleasures on hold.

Prayerfully seek out a meeting place for you and the Lord. Enter this place regularly with a spirit of expectation to receive a Divine download. Bring something to record what you hear.

Be open for different experiences while in this place. There may be times when you cry in the fetal position. Other times you might sing. Perhaps you will sit, stand, kneel, or lay out flat. You may have times where you enter and leave your dedicated place with no clear evidence of any change at all.

No time spent in the presence of the Lord is wasted time. God will honor your faithfulness in ways you cannot imagine. Seek out an accountability partner to encourage your faithfulness in your time with the Lord.

Mirror Moment
Am I committed to setting aside time for the Lord even in seasons when I cannot hear his voice or feel his presence?

Discernment - The Results

Discernment enables you to maintain more of a proactive rather than reactive position to the affairs of life. When you can identify the real threat in your seasons of opposition, you are able to apply the most optimal strategy for removing it. Your discernment is the channel through which you can hear from God and determine whether your decisions are in line with His next for your life.

Mirror Moment
Am I allowing God to influence my response to the challenges in my life?

Let Your Crack Show

The Milestone of Evangelism

Come, see a man, which told me all things that ever I did: is not this the Christ?
St. John 4:29

The brokenness of your past is a critical part of your life story.
My Daily Life Coach

Have you ever broken something, and continued to use it? Though, it was not in the condition of its original purchase, you still saw usable value in its broken condition. As you continued to benefit from the use of the broken product, the fact that it was broken, no longer mattered as much or even at all to you.

Isn't it interesting how this concept plays out in the Christian experience? Regardless the level of carelessness or carefulness with which you handle your roles and responsibilities, life can collide with you in such a manner, that you are left in a state of irreparable brokenness.

The remarkable reality in this matter is experienced when you hear God say "bring me your broken pieces."

God's desire for wholeness in your life has never changed. It is often in your state of brokenness, where the power of God is most apparent. In fact, His strength is perfected in your weakness.[1] He is holding you when you cannot hold yourself. He's holding your family together. He's holding your finances together. He's holding your mind together. It is interesting what He does in those seasons; He puts you back together in a manner that the cracks of your catastrophes remain visible.

In doing so, He redefines the wholeness that we once had. Your brokenness is a critical part of your life story. However, even more important was the process by which God put you back together again. The crack remains as a reminder to you and a witness to others of God's power to restore.

Lord, help me to see the value of the scars that are part of my life story.

Evangelism - The Meaning

Evangelism is spreading the Christian gospel through public preaching or personal witness. Every believer has been deputized to function in this capacity. The pulpit of evangelism is not limited to the walls of your place of worship. In fact, it is not stationary, it is mobile and exists wherever you are.

The diversity that exists within the harvest of those to whom you are called, means that the same approach may not work for all audiences. So effective evangelism is achieved through both your message as well as your methods.

Mirror Moment
How can I share the gospel more effectively to the audiences in my sphere of influence?

Evangelism - The Calling

But sanctify the Lord God in your hearts: and be ready always to give an answer to every man that asketh you a reason of the hope that is in you with meekness and fear:　　　　　*I Peter 3:15*

Qualification is not based on Christian longevity or pedigree. God can use anyone, and He desires to use everyone in relationship with Him to compel[2] others to experience God for themselves. Private communion with God does not replace your call to use the public platforms He provides to speak up and to speak out to others concerning the hope you have in Him.

Mirror Moment
As it relates to my relationship with God, how would I describe the balance between my private reflection and public testimony?

Evangelism - The Challenges

Evangelism requires you to overcome both the mirror and the mirage. The mirror speaks of the inadequacies you harbor about yourself; what you see when you look at yourself, and not the truth that God sees. The mirage speaks of the false assumptions that you make of the audience to which you are called; "they don't want this," "they are fine with the way they are," "they will reject me and the message."

Struggling with the call of evangelism places you in good company. Many of those whom God used mightily in His word not only encountered the same struggles but also witnessed the blessing of saying yes to God, that was waiting for them on the other side of the struggle.

Mirror Moment
Is my greatest challenge to personal evangelism, my perceived personal inadequacies or the fear of rejection?

Evangelism - The Process

The first step in the process of evangelism is to develop a habit of spending time with God. Drawing others to Christ is not about who you are; it is about the work you allow God to do in you as you sit at his feet. Notice in the opening scripture that the woman's unsavory reputation likely caused her to be ostracized in her community. Yet, after spending time with Jesus; allowing him to speak life into the desperate, broken and lonely places in her heart, she was able to stand before her community in such a compelling fashion that they left what they were doing and followed her to Jesus.

This is the reason why God desires to give you more than you can handle;[3] so the excess can be poured into the lives of others. Yes, your life speaks louder than your words, but your life doesn't replace your responsibility to use your words. Evangelism does not require a seminary degree or a clergy collar. All it really requires is a testimony. "Look at what God has done for me." "The same joy, the same peace, the same freedom that I am experiencing is awaiting you on the other side of your yes."

Mirror Moment
How am I handling the overflow of what God is pouring into my life?

Evangelism - The Results

And I, if I be lifted up from the earth, will draw all men unto me.

St. John 12:32

Evangelism offers the only hope for a hopeless generation. This passage from St. John parallels a similar account in Numbers 21 where the people of God were bitten by snakes in the wilderness. Moses made a snake out of brass and put it on a high pole such that when the people looked at it, their lives were spared. Unlike silver or gold, brass is an impure metal and can therefore be likened to sin. Just like the snake in the wilderness, when Jesus who was sinless, was lifted up on the cross of Calvary, He took on the sin of the world and became the answer for all sinners. Through evangelism, we are once again pointing people to the only hope of freedom from the poisonous bondage of sin.

Mirror Moment
What has been the result of me placing my hope and faith in Jesus Christ?

Raise Your
Expectations
The Milestone of Expectation

Meanwhile, the boat was far out to sea when the wind came up against them and they were battered by the waves. At about four o'clock in the morning, Jesus came toward them walking on the water. They were scared out of their wits. "A ghost!" they said, crying out in terror. But Jesus was quick to comfort them. "Courage, it's me. Don't be afraid."   *Matthew 14:24-27 (MSG)*

Peace is not found in the absence of conflict; rather it is found in the presence of Christ.   *My Daily Life Coach*

If you were to list the elements that make for a good motion picture thriller, what would they be? Perhaps your list would include the creativity of the plot, the cast of characters, the setting of the scenes, and the provocative nature of the music and sound effects. Whereas all of these components are integral to the quality of the film, would you agree that there is one central component that must be in place to make your viewing experience worthwhile: the element of surprise?

You know, that edge of your seat, shoulder jerking, heart pounding feeling that you get when something you didn't expect suddenly happens. Who's going to jump out from around the corner? What object is going to crash through the window? Whose hand will suddenly be laid on the back shoulder of the character who is walking cautiously forward? It is the unpredictability of what will happen next that keeps the audience awake, engaged, and wanting more.

It's not hard to see the parallel between the fantasy of this experience and the reality of the Christian experience. Walking by faith, means you never know what is going to happen next. What will be the result of the pregnancy test? What will be the result of my blood work? Will I get the job or the promotion? However, like the central character in a thriller, you have the confidence that through everything that happens you are going to emerge from the darkness of uncertainty to a place of triumph.

The opening passage is one of the many thrillers that Jesus introduced into the lives of His disciples. After the miracle of the feeding of 5000 men, Jesus commands His disciples to board a boat and sail to the other side while he stayed behind. While the boat was in the midst of the sea, a storm arose. The disciples experience the element of surprise when, as they were riding through the storm, Jesus appears on the sea walking toward them. His words to the disciples are interesting at this point; "do not be afraid." Do the words of Jesus seem reasonable to you? How could a person not be afraid at such a sight? The answer to this question is simple and can be summed up in one word: expectation.

As far as the disciples knew, Jesus was still back in the place where they left him. Jesus was the last person that they were expecting to see.

Herein lies the issue that Jesus struggled with the most concerning the disciples and even with his people yet today. As you carry out your Divine assignment, through every experience there is one constant that holds; you can "expect" to see the power of God working on your behalf. Regardless how the episodes change, Jesus is always there. Peace is not found in the absence of conflict; rather it is found in the presence of Christ. It is not enough to know that he is there, but you should always expect to see his power displayed in a manner that allows you to walk on top of the waves of your uncertainties and be the threat to that which dares to threaten you.

Lord, help me to sustain the expectation of experiencing your presence in every season of my life.

Expectation - The Meaning

Expectation is confidently awaiting the arrival of an experience. It is the expectation of seeing the hand of God move on your behalf that should keep you moving forward. Expectation is not satisfied with yesterday's revelation of who God is. Instead, your expectation should spring from an understanding that the revelation of God is yet unfolding. Your expectation should be fueled from a desire to see and experience God in new and refreshing ways.

Mirror Moment

How would my attitude change regarding what I am facing now, if I expected to see the power of God work it out for my good?

Expectation - The Calling

My soul, wait thou only upon God; for my expectation is from him.
He only is my rock and my salvation: he is my defense; I shall not be
moved.   *Psalm 62:5-6*

Expectation is the call to establish stability in God alone; to say with the Psalmist, "He only is my rock." God is the only eternal constant. He is, who he has always been, and always will be. When heaven and earth has passed away, God will still be God.

Consequently, He is the only true source of reliability. He desires to show up in your life in ways you couldn't have imagined. Walking with God means you must expect to be expanded. His desire is not to surprise you as much as it is to expand your understanding of who He is.

So, the call of expectation is to keep the antenna of your consciousness raised, the door of your heart opened, and the readiness of your feet primed to step into the waves with the Lord.

Mirror Moment
Am I satisfied with yesterday's revelation of who God is, or am I
expecting to know Him more?

Expectation - The Challenges

But when he saw the wind boisterous, he was afraid; and beginning to sink, he cried, saying, Lord, save me.   *Matthew 14:30*

Distraction is a major challenge of expectation. Notice in the passage above, that Peter's ability to expect and experience the impossible was based on where his eyes were focused. Desperate times are unavoidable, as are their effect of testing the strength of your resolve to trust God unconditionally.

Sinking is the result of recognizing the limitation of your own efforts and abilities. When faced with difficulty, don't focus on the winds and waves. Instead, speak to them. Settle in your heart that God did not position you to abandon you when you need Him most. Don't limit your confidence of His presence to what you are able to see and feel.

Mirror Moment
Are my distractions doing all the talking, or am I speaking back to them according to God's word?

Expectation - The Process

And they overcame him by the blood of the Lamb, and by the word of their testimony; and they loved not their lives unto the death.

Revelation 12:11

One of the central benefits of your relationships in the body of Christ is sharing testimonies of the power of God. When you can read and hear of how God has worked on behalf of others, it gives you inspiration and insight into what He is able to do for you. Make a list of the times in your life when God defied the odds on your behalf. Keep these before you as a track record of His faithfulness to you.

Mirror Moment
How does God's track record of faithfulness in my life affect my expectation that the same faithfulness will be seen in whatever lies ahead of me?

Expectation - The Results

Living with expectation of seeing God in new and refreshing ways gives you the courage to face anything. It allows you to rely less on your efforts and abilities and more on His. Expectation always gives you something to look forward to in your knowledge of who God is. It allows you to live life beyond your present limitations.

Mirror Moment
Are my perceived limitations a result of my lack of expectation?

Break the Cycle
The Milestone of Freedom

What shall we say then? Shall we continue in sin, that grace may abound? God forbid. How shall we, that are dead to sin, live any longer therein?

Romans 6:1-2

Redirect the energy and creativity that has been invested in that which separates you from God toward that which draws you closer to Him.

My Daily Life Coach

You are caught breaking the law, arrested, and thrown into jail. The weight of your crime has resulted in an exorbitantly high bail being posted for your release. There in the cell of your confinement, you sit in anxiety; imagining what will become of the mess in which you have found yourself. Not an hour later, one of the correctional officers approaches you with the news that your bail has been paid in full, and you are free to go.

You then walk out of the correctional facility and return to the place where you were originally caught, and engage in the same unlawful activity, only to look up and find yourself thrown back into the place of your previous confinement. Except this time, since you are a repeat offender, your bail has now been doubled. Your anxiety now intensifies, as the idea of your release seems even more improbable than the first time. At that moment the same correctional officer approaches you with the same message that you have been released.

Even if you wanted to stop your unlawful activities at this point, what motivation do you have to end this cycle of bondage? It appears that you are free to do as you please without it costing you anything. What do you do when the cautious avoidance of failure has been replaced with a careless interpretation of freedom?

It is to this area of character development that the passage above is speaking. The answer is found in the realization that the freedom to be experienced in the God-direction for my life, always supersedes the bondage to be found in the me-direction for my life. What salvation has rescued you from pales in comparison to the abundant life that it has brought you to.

Redirect the energy and creativity that has been invested in that which separates you from God toward that which draws you closer to Him. This requires consistent intentionality in prayer, study, and fellowship with like-minded individuals. Just like moving closer to the S-u-n, moving closer to the S-o-n melts away the cycle-recurring behaviors that keep you locked in guilt and bondage.

Lord, help me to break out of the cycle of bondage and to move in the God-direction for my life.

Freedom - The Meaning

Freedom is release from the restraints that hinder or prevent living life to its full. Unlike the internal freedom that only God provides, external freedom rooted in the lures and promises of this world have an expiration date.

Note that true freedom, which proceeds from God, is not the same as the prostituted, used, misused, abused, and thrown away, freedom of this world. True freedom exists within the boundary lines of God's purpose. It is restrained; not with cords of God's control of me, but with cords of my commitment to Him for posting the bail for my soul. He freed me, not to control my actions, but to capture my heart.

Mirror Moment

Am I handling my freedom as a prostitute or honoring it as a spouse?

Freedom - The Calling

For, brethren, ye have been called unto liberty; only use not liberty
for an occasion to the flesh, but by love serve one another.

Galatians 5:13

The calling of freedom is a calling to service. Not to serve the needs of your own pursuits, but the requirements of God's calling. There is no greater freedom than that to be experienced while walking in the calling of God. This calling is not exclusive. God wants everyone to be free! The calling of freedom is relentless. Our failures did not forfeit His passion to pay the price for our freedom.

Mirror Moment
How am I using my freedom to serve the calling God has for my life?

Freedom - The Challenges

Significant challenges associated with walking in true freedom include: The pride of control, the abandonment of Divine responsibility and the presumption of endless rescues.

The pride of control is when I deem myself as responsible in any extent for the freedom I possess. When I feel like I am responsible for my freedom, I convince myself that I can handle it in a manner that advances me, even if that comes at the expense of hurting others.

What's worse is when I look up from the bottom of the pit that my pride has led to and have the audacity to look for God to swing in and save the day as He has so many times before. When will I honor God as the source of my freedom? When will I return to the post to which He has assigned me? When will I stop prostituting his grace with my disobedience?

Mirror Moment
How am I using my freedom to honor God, rather than to advance my own agenda?

Freedom - The Process

In ancient eastern times there was a watchman that stood in a high tower in the city for the purpose of sounding the alarm when danger was on the horizon. He didn't wait until danger arrived at the city gates. Rather the call was made while the danger was off in the distance. The effectiveness of this strategy was determined by the position of the guard.

Likewise, you are not called to sea level thinking; you are called to elevated thinking. Only when your mind is elevated, can you experience true freedom. Man can hurt your body and remove your possessions, but if you have your mind you always have a bridge to experience more freedom than those who are trying to keep you in bondage.

Mirror Moment
What are the weights that are limiting the elevation of my mind, and what can I do to address them?

Freedom - The Results

Freedom allows me to maintain the proper perspective regardless of my circumstances. Freedom is God's design for my life. No satisfaction surpasses that of being in the perfect will of God. True freedom filters the voices that influence my life. Before I allow anything that I hear to enter my heart, it must line up with what God says concerning me in his word.

Mirror Moment
What voices do I entertain that are limiting the freedom God desires for my life?

Reach Beyond Your Now

The Milestone of Hope

This I recall to my mind, therefore have I hope. It is of the Lord's mercies that we are not consumed, because his compassions fail not. They are new every morning: great is thy faithfulness.

Lamentations 3:21-23

There is more in store for your than what is presently in front of you.

My Daily Life Coach

What is it that has you overwhelmed right now? Can you identify it? Perhaps you struggle to put it into words. Is it more than just one thing? Is it easier to describe the way it makes you feel? Tired. Restless. Angry. Stressed. Anxious. Confused. Self-conscious. Embarrassed. Ashamed. Do any of these emotional conditions resonate with you? If so, there is good news; you are normal. Never was there a person who lived an entire life without having to encounter the emotional rollercoasters that accompany it. Your life story will be comprised of highs, lows, and in-betweens.

You have the God-given right to have an authentic human response to the ever-changing affairs of your life.

Don't feel guilty for being human. Your emotions reflect your relationship to yourself. Your spirit reflects your relationship to God. What you receive through the channel of your spirit, should always take priority over what you receive through the channel of your emotions. For it is what you receive through the channel of the spirit that enables you to press through, to heal from, and to grow up, regardless of what life throws your way.

This is what we see in the opening scripture. Amid the dam-breaking, tidal wave of his emotions, Jeremiah still left the channel of his spirit open to communicate to his mind concerning the faithfulness of his God. This is what sustained him. This is what encouraged him to press on. This is what allowed him to see how he was feeling, in context, instead of allowing it to be in control. Likewise, through the eyes of your spirit, you too can look beyond what you are presently facing.

You too can see the faithfulness of God's provision and protection. God has a way of reminding you that your condition is not your conclusion. That there is more in store for you than what is presently in front of you. This is your confidence. This is your hope. This is the anchor that keeps the winds of your emotions from throwing you off course of the plans that God has in store for you. Always allow your hope in God to stabilize your emotions.

Lord, help me to sustain a vibrant hope in your promises for my life.

Hope - The Meaning

Hope is a sustained, optimistic, outlook that reaches beyond your present circumstances. It does not ignore what you are facing, nor prevent your human response to it. However, hope allows you to keep your affairs in the context of the bigger picture of God's better for your life.

Hope is your down payment on God's destiny for you. Like a bridge that connects two towering mountains, the integrity of your hope determines whether you reach or fall short of what God has in store for your life. Hope views whatever is presently in front of you as a steppingstone that takes you higher and moves you closer to God's next for your life.

Mirror Moment

Am I regarding the challenges that I am currently facing as steppingstones or stumbling blocks?

Hope - The Calling

But let us, who are of the day, be sober, putting on the breastplate of faith and love; and for an helmet, the hope of salvation.

I Thessalonians 5:8

The calling of hope is to protect your mind. Don't allow anything to alter the vision that God has given you concerning your future. Allow the volume of his voice to drown out any voices that are contrary to it.

The calling of hope is for you to sustain the assurance of your position in Christ despite the ever-changing seasons of your life. You can ride through any storm if you are riding with Jesus. You are who God says you are. You have what God says you have. You will be what God says you will be. For if God be for you, who can be against you. If you walk with him, the only way that you can fail is for his word to fail.

Mirror Moment
What efforts am I making to protect my mind?

Hope - The Challenges

Rejoicing in hope; patient in tribulation; continuing instant in prayer;
Romans 12:12

Impatience sits among the top challenges that seek to threaten your hope. Hope, by its very nature implies that you do not have it yet; that there is a period between the inception and the reality of what you desire. Waiting isn't fun. In fact, it can be very frustrating and discouraging, especially when you see other people in the place where you desire to be. Or when God's timetable doesn't line up with yours. You thought it through. You planned it out. You're doing all the right things and avoiding the wrong things. What gives?

Take some hints from the passage above. Nothing fuels hope like praise. God inhabits the praise of his people. Praising God in your time of waiting, is like blowing air into a flat tire. It lifts your head and reminds you of God's track record; that He's always been there. He's always provided just what you need. His timing is perfect, and his promises are true. Your hope is in his word and his word cannot fail.

Mirror Moment
While I am waiting for what I desire, am I displaying an attitude that invites and honors God?

Hope - The Process

Now faith is the substance of things hoped for, the evidence of things not seen.   *Hebrews 11:1*

So how can you grow in your hope? A good starting point is to recognize that your hope should not be rooted in your emotions, it should be rooted in the knowledge of God's word. Hope is not about how you feel as much as it is what you know as a believer.

What has God said in his word about your situation? What has he spoken in your spirit that gives you the confidence that there's got to be more than this? Hold on to that word no matter what.

Another thing to consider, is that faith is the hands of your hope. That is what the passage above is saying. Hope without evidence and substance is not hope at all. You are not hoping for a job if you do not put in an application. You are not hoping to improve your health if you continue to engage in unhealthy behaviors. What you are hoping for will not occur in the absence of your involvement.

Mirror Moment
How does my lifestyle feed or starve my hope?

Hope - The Results

Hope gives purpose, aim, and direction to your life. It sustains a sense of optimism in you, amid the ever-changing seasons of your life. Hope reminds you of God's promises, and inspires you to stay on track to experience them.

Hope moves you into action to design your life in a fashion that pleases God. Hope filters out the forces that threaten it and gravitates toward the people, the opportunities, and the environments that give it life.

Mirror Moment
Am I feeding my hope with my emotions, or with God's promises?

Fix the Flat
The Milestone of Inspiration

And the Lord God formed man of the dust of the ground, and breathed into his nostrils the breath of life; and man became a living soul.

Genesis 2:7

Anything outside of or apart from the word of God is either dead or dying."

My Daily Life Coach

How do you remain inspired in circumstances that lack inspiration? Is it even possible to do so? Can you recall a time when your level of inspiration was at an all-time low? Is there anything that you could have said or done differently to prevent that from happening?

To answer these questions, it's helpful to understand the origin of the word, inspire. It comes from a Latin word meaning to blow into or breathe upon. Interesting enough, you will notice that the first occurrence of this is found in the creation of man.

God formed man from the dust of the earth and breathed into him the breath of life. It was only then that man became alive.

Without the breath of God, we are nothing more than perishable empty shells, born with a predetermined expiration date. It is only through the breath of God that you can experience life. Anything outside of or apart from God is either dead or dying.

Your inspiration should not be rooted in the volatility of your emotions. Herein lies the power of the word of God; instead of embracing the lies of your emotions, you can place your emotions on the life support of the word. By doing so, you'll find that inspiration transcends any circumstance; that even in the darkest night of the soul, inspiration is available and can be accessed and enjoyed by the person who opens the floodgates of God's word.

The word of God leaves us without excuse to live beyond circumstantial inspiration. The source of your supply lives inside of you.[1] Why remain thirsty when all you need to do is take a drink from the well that never runs dry.

Lord, help me to recognize and access your inspiration in every season of my life

Inspiration - The Meaning

Inspiration is the drive, the enthusiasm, the passion with which an activity is carried out. It answers the question "why;" "Why did I get out of the bed this morning," "Why do I continue to face the challenges in the workplace or the classroom," "Why do I continue to exercise and eat right," Why do I resist that which goes against the grain of God's will for my life?" None of these choices occur in the absence of an intentional effort or inspiration.

Mirror Moment
As it relates to the areas in my life where I am most engaged or committed, what is my why?

Inspiration - The Calling

Have I not commanded you? Be strong and courageous. Do not be afraid; do not be discouraged, for the LORD your God will be with you wherever you go."

Joshua 1:9

The calling of inspiration is futuristic in nature. Not only does it address the inspiration-robbers lurking in your current environment, but it also anticipates the hidden, unexpected, "gotchas," that you've yet to encounter. The passage above speaks of the leadership transfer from Moses to Joshua and how Joshua was to respond to the obstacles associated with bringing the nation of Israel into their place of inheritance.

God desires for you to have the same assurance as He did for Joshua; that the God who called you will be with you, as you carry out your assignment. This is the calling of inspiration; for it to be rooted in the assurance of God's presence amid the ever-changing circumstances of your life.

Mirror Moment

How is my inspiration to move forward sustained in the seasons when my faith is tested?

Inspiration - The Challenges

Challenges associated with inspiration include complacency and discouragement. Complacency is experienced when you seek to establish comfort at your current level of success. Pursuing an ever-expanding revelation of the Lord is not solely for your benefit, but also for those God desires to reach through you.

Discouragement is the aftermath of an emotional collision, where you are left to deal with the wreckage resulting from your actions or those of others. The well from which you draw your strength will determine whether you embrace the stagnation of discouragement or the perseverance of inspiration. As was told to the woman at the well, as a child of God, everything you need to fuel your inspiration resides inside of you. If you allow God to fuel your inspiration there will be no aspect of his purpose for your life, that you will not be able to achieve?

Mirror Moment
How am I managing the threats of discouragement and complacency to my inspiration?

Inspiration - The Process

Kool-Aid was one of my favorite beverages as a child. Not only was it tasty, but it was extremely easy to make. All it would require was a gallon of water, the Kool-Aid mix of my choosing, and sugar. There was a three-step process to the enjoyment of this beverage, pouring, stirring, and drinking. Leaving any part out would be detrimental to the experience.

Such is the case with inspiration. You must remain in a place where the word is poured into you. You must then refuse to allow it to settle in the insignificant and forgotten places of your mind, but you must engage the word until its contents cover and are suspended throughout your entire heart. Such engagement serves to renew your desire and embolden your courage to continue moving in the God direction for your life.

Mirror Moment
How am I stirring up and engaging the word that is in my heart?

Inspiration - The Results

When your inspiration is sourced from the word of God it changes your concept of winning in life. Your sense of fulfillment is not based on your desire for situation-specific outcomes. Rather it rests solely in the answer to the question, "Was God pleased with how I managed that situation?" How do I know that God was pleased? Because the word fueled my faith to persevere. What pleases God is not the outcome of my efforts, but the faith that I maintained through the process, independent of the outcome.

Mirror Moment
What does winning in life look like to me?

Keep Asking Questions
The Milestone of Investigation

But without faith it is impossible to please him: for he that cometh to God must believe that he is, and that he is a rewarder of them that diligently seek him.

Hebrews 11:6

You have not been sentenced to the paralysis of confusion concerning your purpose.

My Daily Life Coach

You are not an afterthought in the mind of God. Your existence is by His Divine intention. This reality can be seen even from your inception. Medical science suggests that the odds were stacked against you at the time of your birth, yet you made it! Not only did you make it then, but you have been kept through all the highs, lows, and in-betweens of your life up to this point.

You must be special! Jeremiah 1:4 opens with the words, "then the word of the Lord came to me..." Isn't it interesting how God pursues after us? He is so interested in you knowing who you are, that He does not leave you to figure it out on your own.

Nor does He wait for you to pursue after Him. Your purpose is pursuing you. God is not the author of confusion.[1] You have not been sentenced to the paralysis of confusion concerning your purpose.

It's okay to have questions concerning your identity and calling. Faith is required to please God.[2] Having all the answers, eliminates the need for faith. Questions are often your greatest gifts. God uses them to bring you to where He is. No matter how close you are to God, you can always move a little closer. Each question is an opportunity to take a deeper step in the God direction for your life.

Lord, help me to remain in pursuit of your direction for my life.

Investigation - The Meaning

Investigation is the gathering of information to arrive at the right conclusion. It involves laying aside subjective thoughts and views to achieve objective conclusions. Investigation is a central milestone for all believers. Your personal relationship with God through Jesus Christ is a cordial invitation to a growth journey in the knowledge of who He is and what He requires from your life.

Mirror Moment

What does my level of investigation and pursuit of the Lord, reveal about the sincerity of my walk with Him?

Investigation - The Calling

Ask, and it shall be given you; seek, and ye shall find; knock, and it shall be opened unto you: For every one that asketh receiveth; and he that seeketh findeth; and to him that knocketh it shall be opened.

Matthew 7:7-8

Investigation is the calling to allow what you are searching for, to begin and end in God. This means that God should be at the core of your quest for answers and direction. The worst thing you could do is eliminate God from your process of discovery. This doesn't mean that you will obtain the answers that you seek when or in the manner that you desire to have them. It may not immediately be apparent to you, but God always desires the best outcome for your life. Receive his direction and his answers. Reject all alternatives.

Mirror Moment
How am I maintaining the confidence that God desires the best outcome for me, even in the dark, lonely, and confusing seasons of my life?

Investigation - The Challenges

Jesus saith unto him, I am the way, the truth, and the life: no man
cometh unto the Father, but by me. *John 14:6*

A central challenge associated with investigation is learning how to prioritize truth over facts. Facts are significant, but truth is essential. The facts may provide a prognosis, but truth can provide the cure. Facts may identify trends and patterns, but truth can break the cycle. Facts may see locked doors, but truth can provide the keys to open them. Always review the facts through the lens of the truth of God's word. Allow His truth to have the final say.

Mirror Moment
How well do I hold on to God's truth, when it is different from the
facts that are directly in front of me?

Investigation - The Process

That they should seek the Lord, if haply they might feel after him,
and find him, though he be not far from every one of us:
For in him we live, and move, and have our being; as certain also of
your own poets have said, For we are also his offspring.

Acts 17:27-28

The process of investigation begins with the humility of surrender. In order for your heart to receive the clarity of Divine instruction, you must be willing to clear the road of your own preconceived ideas. When you allow your existence to reside in God, then all your answers are within your reach.

You would likely be amazed at how close you are to the answers that you seek. The Lord knocks at the door of your heart. He does not kick the door in. The door can represent traditional mindsets and limitations to which you have confined yourself. The origins of these doors can trace back to your childhood. Though there is truth to be discovered in what you have received to this point, your partial truth is no substitute for God's holistic and absolute truth. Keep seeking. Keep knocking. You won't be disappointed.

Mirror Moment
What mindsets are restricting me from receiving the truth that God desires for me to walk in?

Investigation - The Results

Investigation yields the fruit of understanding. It places you in a category of the "road less-travelled." Not many are willing to diligently make the necessary spiritual investments for clarity in their decisions. Investigation changes your perspective of the challenges that you must face. It gives you the confidence that you are moving in the God direction for your life.

Mirror Moment
What investments am I making to obtain clarity in my decisions?

Talk to Your Friend
The Milestone of Prayer

Do not be anxious about anything, but in every situation, by prayer and petition, with thanksgiving, present your requests to God.   *Philippians 4:6 (NIV)*

Sleeping the whole day, can do nothing for a soul that is tired.   *My Daily Life Coach*

Where is your happy place? Is it at home; working in your yard or hanging out in your man cave or lady's lair? Is it at the mall, searching for the best sales, or at the gym burning off the stress and sweating away the cares of the day. Does it require a distant drive, a flight, or cruise to sandy beaches or majestic mountains. Wherever it is, what makes this your happy place? Does it provide for you a sense of emotional therapy; an escape from the demands of adulting, solving problems, performing on the job, changing diapers, cooking, cleaning, studying, or struggling to make ends meet?

Your happy place is the sanctuary that relaxes and refuels you to manage the affairs of your life. Though it is good to have a physical happy place, even more important is to have a spiritual happy place; a place of prayer, where you can go 24 and 7 in full expectation of meeting a God who loves to both hear from, and speak to you.

The place of prayer, yields for you what no other place can provide. Other places offer only a temporary sense of satisfaction, but they can do nothing for a heart that is weak or broken. Sleeping the whole day, can do nothing for a soul that is tired. God wants you to be restored in every area of your life.

Prayer is the place where the presence of God is experienced. It may not always give you goosebumps or bring you to tears of joy, but rest assured that no time that you devote to God, is wasted time. He is moving on your behalf, and in the behalf of those that you bring before Him, even if it is not immediately evident. Establish a practice, a discipline, a habit, a routine of spending time in the place of prayer.

Lord, help me to maintain a lifestyle of prayer.

Prayer - The Meaning

Prayer is a conversation with God where He hears you, speaks to you, and transforms you. Sometimes it requires that you speak, other times no words are necessary. It has no required time limit and can cover topics that range from life's deepest questions to matters of little consequence. Prayer is about hearing God, listening to his thoughts, and catching a glimpse of his heart. Prayer is the privilege of touching the heart of God. This triggers Him to act on your behalf, yielding unmistakable transformation in your life and in the lives of those that you bring before Him. Developing a prayer life causes you to follow God's leadership, and to develop a purposeful life that honors Him.

Mirror Moment
What are some ways that I can become more intentional about regularly setting aside time for God in prayer?

Prayer - The Calling

Pray without ceasing. I Thessalonians 5:17

The calling of prayer is to maintain ongoing communication with the Lord. Having a personal relationship with God, means that you do not have to wait for a certain time or until you are in a certain place, to speak to or hear from Him. You can take Him to school, to work, to the store, or wherever you are. God wants to hear from you. God has a word for you. His calendar is always free. His ears are always open. His undivided attention is always available.

Mirror Moment
How can I become more comfortable with speaking to the Lord whenever I want, and wherever I am?

Prayer - The Challenges

A central challenge to maintaining a lifestyle of prayer, can be seen in how you manage the competing priorities in your life. There is no need in saying, "once I complete this", or "get past that", or "figure out the other," "then I will be ready to devote more time to prayer".

Life happens. There is always going to be another bill to pay, or problem to solve, or something else that is going to fight for the seat of your priority and focus. Prayer makes God's presence more real in your life. He doesn't want you to figure out your challenges and then bring whatever energy you have left to him in prayer.

God wants to do life with you. He desires to stand with, fight with, cry with, and rejoice with you amid the torrents of your life. Stop treating prayer as an afterthought. Talk to the Lord throughout your day. Invite his presence, his counsel, and his wisdom into every decision from the menial to the complex.

Mirror Moment
Do I manage my prayer life, amid my competing priorities, in a manner that honors God?

Prayer - The Process

After this manner therefore pray ye: Our Father which art in heaven,
Hallowed be thy name. Thy kingdom come. Thy will be done in earth,
as it is in heaven. Give us this day our daily bread. And forgive us our
debts, as we forgive our debtors. And lead us not into temptation, but
deliver us from evil: For thine is the kingdom, and the power, and the
glory, forever. Amen. *Matthew 6:9-13*

In the passage above, Jesus lays out the blueprint of seven key components of a prayer life that honor God; relationship, jurisdiction, worship, divine purpose, divine provision, forgiveness, and divine covering.

It opens with the words "Our Father." Here Jesus is emphasizing relationship. He knows you more than you know yourself, so you can be transparent before Him. Prayer is the place where guilt and shame can be abandoned. Hiding and keeping your faults in the dark, prevents them from being transformed by the power of God.

Jesus then says, "Which art in heaven." Here Jesus is emphasizing the jurisdiction of God; that you can rest assured that any challenge on your heart, is under His feet. There is nothing too hard for you and God to handle together.

Next Jesus says, "Hallowed be thy Name." Here Jesus is emphasizing worship. In His presence, you are standing on holy ground. Pause to recognize and acknowledge who God is; that he alone is holy, that he alone is worthy, and that there is none like Him in all the earth.

Jesus then says, Thy Kingdom come, thy will be done in earth as it is in heaven. Here Jesus is emphasizing Divine Purpose; that whatever personal request or agenda you are bringing to Him in prayer, His will is what matters, His purpose is what takes priority.

99

Prayer - The Process

Jesus then says, Give us this day our daily bread. Here Jesus is emphasizing Divine Provision; that you should recognize and acknowledge that all you have by way of health, wealth, or influence is the result of what God has provided for you.

Jesus then says, "forgive us our debts as we forgive our debtors." Here Jesus is emphasizing forgiveness; that we should not enter his presence without the willingness to forgive those whose words or actions have caused us pain.

Jesus then says, "Lead us not into temptation, but deliver us from evil." Here Jesus is emphasizing Divine Covering; that you should pray that the Lord covers and protects you from any force that would threaten your walk with Him.

Write these components down. Try to incorporate them into your prayer life and experience the presence and the power of God in new and refreshing ways. Knowing what the Word says enables you to frame your prayers appropriately. Spending time in the Word increases your ability to determine God's will and to hear His voice concerning the specific matters in your life. Praying according to God's Word and His will ensures that your motives will be pure.

Mirror Moment
What are the major hinderances to my consistency of spending personal time with God?

Prayer - The Results

A lifestyle of prayer is the key to good emotional health and spirituality. Prayer brings about transformation in your life and in the lives of those you bring before the Lord. Prayer provides you with a place where your guilt and your shame can be abandoned.

You can be transparent in the presence of a God who knows you more than you know yourself and is not surprised by your missteps, nor does this impact his love for you. Prayer gives you the opportunity to work in cooperation with God to do his will. As his chosen vessel, His power works through your hands, spreads through your feet, and speaks through your mouth, resulting in the expansion of His kingdom in the earth.

Mirror Moment

How does knowing the results of a healthy prayer life influence the investment that I am willing to put into my own?

Speak Truth to Power
The Milestone of Prophecy

God hath spoken once; twice have I heard this; that power belongeth unto God.   *Psalm 62:11*

It is wonderful to be inspired from the word of God. It is completely different to call upon that inspiration when met with theheat of difficult situations.

My Daily Life Coach

Do you remember your high school math teachers; how easy they made the problems look when they worked them out, step by step in the classroom? You took great notes and convinced yourself that you understood the concepts that were presented.

Later that evening you sat down and started your homework and came across a similar problem as was worked out in the classroom. You cracked your knuckles and charged right in with an unapologetically cocky, "I got this," attitude.

However, despite the notes you took and the confidence that you experienced earlier, you found yourself struggling with the problem at hand.

This scenario presents us with one of the most prevailing realities of the Christian experience and life as a whole; the distinction between theory and practice; between information received and information applied. It is wonderful to be inspired from the word of God. It is completely different to call upon that inspiration when met with the heat of difficult situations. Sometimes you can't help but feel outnumbered; as though you've been set up; that nobody warned you it would be this difficult, it would require this much, and it would take this long.

In these seasons there is a direct relationship between your survival and your perspective. The overwhelming nature of difficult times comes because of how they touch you; you can actually feel the weight of the load, the heat of the flame, and the pain of the wound. One of the most critical principles for you to maintain in these seasons is that all power is delegated by God for His purpose.

On His way to the cross, Pilate told Jesus, "I have the power to crucify you, or to release you." To which Jesus responded, "You could have no power, except it were given from above.[1]"
Jesus teaches us that by speaking truth to power, we are reminding its possessors of the source from which all power comes. God has a purpose for any power that He releases. Who is your Pilate today? Is it a physical, spiritual, or financial condition that seeks to strike fear in you? Prophesy to your antagonist today that power belongs to God and that He will ultimately use all power to advance his purpose and bring glory to his name.

Lord, help me to maintain the right perspective
concerning the difficult seasons of my life."

Prophecy - The Meaning

Prophecy is a unique platform to which the Lord has called you. It is a platform that boldly speaks out and denounces anything that challenges the truth of God's word. Consequently, it is not a platform of popularity and esteem.

In the Old Testament, it was typically not a time to celebrate when they saw the prophet coming, as they knew there would be a word from the Lord that would challenge lifestyles and mindsets that were against the will of the Lord.

It is an unfortunate reality that truth is typically not popular in this age. Prophecy is the legacy of the believer; to raise your voice like a trumpet and declare the truth that sets the captive free.

Mirror Moment
How does God feel about the manner in which I am using my voice?

Prophecy - The Calling

And he said unto them, Go ye into all the world, and preach the gospel
to every creature.   *Mark 16:15*

Did you know that a ministry license is not required to share the good news of the gospel? Another word for preach is proclaim. It is communicating with conviction and confidence the greatest demonstration of love that the world has ever witnessed. It is the life-changing power of believing that this was done on your behalf to seal an eternal relationship and fellowship with the lover of your soul.

The life-changing aspect of this experience is what draws the line in the sand between that which pleases and displeases God. This life-changing aspect is what emboldens you to be ready with an answer concerning the hope that lies inside of you[2] and how others can experience this same hope. This life-changing aspect empowers you to live a life that demonstrates the hope that you proclaim.

Mirror Moment
Does my life point those around me to the God who has transformed
it?

Prophecy - The Challenges

From that time many of his disciples went back, and walked no more with him.

John 6:66

Contrary to popular opinion, communicating truth is not the road to rock star status. Truth is not popular, because it challenges the cultures and mindsets of this world. It challenges your own mindset and traditions.

Only when you allow truth to stretch out in your mind and to transform your life, can you expect to see the same transformation in the lives of those in your sphere of influence. It's lonely at the top. Speaking truth may result in standing alone at times.

Your conviction must be stronger than your comfort. Your security can't rest in people. It must rest solely in the God of the truth that you speak. He will never abandon you and He will see to it that the right people are near, not only for you to strengthen, but from whom you can also be strengthened and restored.

Mirror Moment
How would I describe the quality of my courage to do and say what's right even if it results in seasons of loneliness and isolation?

Prophecy - The Process

Prophecy involves speaking up and speaking out. Its effectiveness is tied to a boldness which is grounded in something beyond yourself. Not only does God defend the truth that He calls you to speak, but He is the very essence of that truth.

Spending intentional and consistent time with God is essential. It is not enough to know what to say, but it is just as important to know how God wants you to communicate it. Don't fall to the temptation of imitating someone else's style or approach. God doesn't make carbon copies; He only makes originals.

You have a style of your own and your style is tailor-made for your audience. Ask God to reveal to you who your audience is. Pray for your audience; sight unseen, that the Lord will prepare their hearts to receive the seed of His truth that He desires to flow through your life as well as from your mouth.

Mirror Moment
How do I feel about the originality of my expression and communication style?

Prophecy - The Results

Prophecy releases truth. Truth results in freedom. Bondage was never God's intention for his people. Whenever Israel was in bondage, he sent his word through prophecy to serve as the key to their deliverance. Just like a key does not unlock a door by itself, truth does not bring about freedom to those who are bound independent of their involvement.

God's truth knocks at the doors of the hearts of men, it does not let itself in. Only when the door is opened, and truth is embraced will the chains of sin be replaced with the favor of God.

Mirror Moment

How would my approach to prophecy change if I viewed the words that I spoke as the keys to unlock the doors of bondage to those who heard them?

Live on Purpose
The Milestone of Purpose

For to me to live is Christ, and to die is gain.

Philippians 1:21

We are not to be driven by worthy causes but rather by Divine calling.

My Daily Life Coach

Do you consider yourself successful? If so, then what are the markers of your success? Isn't it easy to fall into the mindset that views success as the target practice of personal pursuits and ambitions; that success is the extent to which you meet the milestones along the trajectory of a life that you have envisioned for yourself? These can be milestones of marriage and family or education and career advancement or even service and legacy.

Whereas each of these are meaningful, central to the Christian experience is the understanding that life was not intended to be a smorgasbord of meaningful pursuits.

We are not to be driven by worthy causes but rather by Divine calling. Don't wait, as did Paul, to get knocked off the high horse[1] of your own pursuits and ambitions, to discover the joy of living on purpose. It is interesting to consider how many people struggle with the concept of purpose. Do you know what your purpose is? As much as this question can have the tendency to catch you off guard, for the child of God, the answer is rather simple.

In the opening passage, Paul makes the answer to this question quite clear in his statement, "to live is Christ." There is no question that the work of Christ was successful. So, what was the key to Christ's success? The bookends of Christ's ministry, from baptism to crucifixion were that, at all costs, He pleased the Father. Herein lies the measuring stick of true success; the confidence that the Father is pleased with my life.

Don't wait until you find your purpose and calling, to please God by operating in it. For it works in reverse; it is your relentless pursuit of pleasing God that brings you into your purpose and calling.

Lord, let my desire the please you, drive me in the direction of your purpose for my life.

Purpose - The Meaning

Your purpose is your life's contribution to the world in which you live. It is influenced by how you were raised as well as the culture to which you have been exposed. So, you should not feel any regret or remorse for any aspect of your life to this point, for your past will feed into your purpose going forward.

A good purpose for your life is not necessarily a God purpose for your life. If you pursue God, good will follow. This doesn't work the other way around.

Mirror Moment
Do I seek to manage my possessions and opportunities in a manner that pleases God, and am I comfortable with anything short of this?

Purpose - The Calling

To everything there is a season, and a time to every purpose under the heaven: *Ecclesiastes 3:1*

The child of God is called to recognize the dynamic and evolving nature of purpose; that purpose has seasons, and the expectations for the same purpose may vary depending on the season at hand.

The calling of purpose is to remain sensitive to the voice of God and to avoid the temptation of "figuring it out." The calling of purpose is to remain in the pursuit of pleasing God, who desires for you to experience the ever-unfolding revelation of who He is, and what He desires to do through your life.

Mirror Moment
How well do I adjust to the Lord's ever-expanding expectations of my life?

Purpose - The Challenges

Walking in purpose involves the alignment of your will with the will of God. This can be challenging, as your desired path is likely to avoid many of the obstacle courses required by the less traveled path of following Christ. However, any challenge associated with moving in the God direction for your life is not worthy to be compared with the eternal blessings that result from this choice. Consequently, it is a fruitless pursuit to seek comfort in something that will not last at the expense of forfeiting everlasting life.

Another challenge associated with purpose is avoiding the temptation to skip steps along the journey to operating in it. Each step, each stage, each gain, each loss, that God ordains is conditioning you to handle His next for your life. It can be both a frustrating and embarrassing reality to arrive in a position that you are not ready to handle, because you skipped over or avoided essential lessons at a previous stage of your life.

Mirror Moment
Could I be limiting myself through the tendency to skip steps in my walk with the Lord?

Purpose - The Process

Thy kingdom come, Thy will be done in earth, as it is in heaven.

Matthew 6:10

Begin your process of identifying and growing in purpose with the understanding that your purpose is an extension of God's larger purpose in the earth. That your ultimate purpose is to put His purpose on display in your sphere of influence. As such, anything that you feel compelled to do should align with the word of God.

Make a list of your strengths and ask those that are close to you to do the same. Compare the lists and bring them to the Lord in prayer. Search for books that are written around ways to develop in the area of your strengths.

Mirror Moment
What efforts am I making to explore my skills and abilities and to determine how God desires to use them for His purpose?

Purpose - The Results

Your purpose is the oxygen of your soul. Regardless of your wealth or accomplishments, the suffocating effects of living apart from your purpose will always limit the quality of your life as it was intended by God.

When you walk in purpose, you make your contribution to expanding God's kingdom. You give others an opportunity to see God through the way He uses you.

Purpose gives you an opportunity to demonstrate to God how much you love and appreciate him, and to be rewarded for your faithfulness to what he has entrusted into your hand.

Mirror Moment
Am I intentional about positioning God in the equation of my success?

Make the Most of It
The Milestone of Stewardship

For the kingdom of heaven is as a man travelling into a far country, who called his own servants, and delivered unto them his goods. And unto one he gave five talents, to another two, and to another one; to every man according to his several ability; and straightway took his journey.

Matthew 25:14-15

Service precedes promotion.

My Daily Life Coach

Have you ever made it to the checkout line at a store, and the cashier recommended a way for you to purchase additional items at a discount? Sounded good right? So good, that you took advantage of the opportunity, only to recognize that doing so, resulted in you spending more money that day than you originally intended. You went in to purchase one thing, and ended up paying more, to take advantage, of the cashier's offer. You have just become the victim of upselling.

One of the central guiding principles in the realm of sales, is to avoid leaving any money on the table.

The key to increasing the profitability of a business, is to take advantage of any opportunity to encourage the customer to spend more. The employee is motivated to make the business more profitable, as it likely yields the benefits of wage increases, security, and better opportunities. Service precedes promotion.

The parallels of this principle are clearly seen in the opening passage. It is the Lord's desire, for you to be blessed. However, He has designed it such that you contribute to the impact of the blessing he has in store for you. God feeds the birds of the air, but He doesn't throw the worms in the nest. The outcome of stewardship is not automatic; it requires work, it requires time, and it requires commitment.

As unnecessary, unfair, and undesirable as this may seem at times, this is God's plan and the reward of doing things God's way far outweighs any struggle that is associated with the journey. You arc more appreciative of the blessings in your life when you have worked hard to obtain them, rather than when they are laid in your lap.

Lord, help me to make the most of all that you have placed in my possession.

Stewardship - The Meaning

The earth is the Lord's, and the fulness thereof; the world, and they that dwell therein.   *Psalm 24:1*

Stewardship is the way a person manages the belongings of another. Just because something is in your possession doesn't mean that it belongs to you. In truth, according to the above passage, nothing belongs to you. Your money doesn't belong to you. Your house and vehicle do not belong to you. The members of your family do not belong to you. Your job and your health do not belong to you. You have been made the steward over these things by the Lord who owns everything. Embracing this mindset is central to experiencing the abundance that God desires for your life.

Mirror Moment
Am I managing what I have been entrusted with in a manner that honors God?

Stewardship - The Calling

As every man hath received the gift, even so minister the same one to another, as good stewards of the manifold grace of God.

I Peter 4:10

The calling of stewardship is to view your possessions as an opportunity to be a blessing to others. As you pour into others, God pours back into you. He is your source. He restores your soul![1]

It's wonderful to be blessed by others. However, God is the source from which all blessing flows. Stop depending on people for that which God alone supplies.

Stewardship is the calling to honor the Lord with what you have been given.[2] Not only did He find you and clean you up. He has hired you to serve in his kingdom with a compensation package that surpasses anything this world could offer.

Mirror Moment
How am I using what I have to be a blessing to others?

Stewardship - The Challenges

Procrastination is a central challenge associated with stewardship; the tendency to plan for a time that is not promised.

Procrastination treats deadlines as moving targets that you are in control of. This is not the case. You serve a God of purpose and timing. Delay results in the waste of time, the waste of treasure, and the loss of impact.

The clock of your stewardship starts now. Don't waste another moment Don't waste another day. Don't waste another opportunity. It's bigger than you. Someone is depending on the contribution that you are called to make. Put down the remote. Turn off your phone. Turn over your plate. Fall on your knees and repent for your detours and delays. Then get up and get busy.

Mirror Moment
What should I be doing now that I have been putting off until later?

Stewardship - The Process

Stewardship requires the setting of realistic goals. If you do not have a target, your shooting is in vain. What are you shooting for? Is it better health, better finances, or stronger relationships? Identify your target and then plan to achieve it.

Stewardship requires shifting from a tactical to a strategic approach to optimizing your resources. Tactical just focuses on getting it done. Strategic focuses on getting it done efficiently and effectively, with minimal waste and optimal results. What kind of improvement do I desire to see? How will I measure the results? Who in my life can I trust to hold me accountable? Stewardship that honors God is not achieved through haphazard apathetic pursuits, but rather through wholehearted focused plans that are birthed out of seeking the Lord.

Mirror Moment
What improvements can I make to the way I manage the resources that God has given me?

Stewardship - The Results

When your stewardship honors God, it yields organic growth in your life. When you optimize what God has given, you never have to worry about receiving more. Good stewardship allows you to witness the power of God in taking a little and multiplying it to become much. It enables you to be a blessing to others and to replicate, in them, the same God-honoring character of strategic thinking, hard work, and commitment.

Mirror Moment
Does my stewardship with what I already have, demonstrate that I am ready for more?

Dance in the Rain
The Milestone of Submission

For as the rain and snow come down from heaven, And do not return there without watering the earth, Making it bear and sprout, And providing seed to the sower and bread to the eater, So will My word be which goes out of My mouth; It will not return to Me void (useless, without result), Without accomplishing what I desire, And without succeeding in the matter for which I sent it.

Isaiah 55:10-11 (AMP)

It is often easier to receive what the word has for you, than what the word requires of you.

My Daily Life Coach

Have you ever noticed how rain has an uncanny way of interrupting your day? Would you agree that it is more common to find yourself running further away from, rather than deeper into, the winds and rains of your physical environment?

The irony of this scenario is that God uses the same rain that you are running away from to produce a harvest, apart from which you cannot live. In essence, you are seeking cover from the same thing that is keeping you alive.

There has never fallen a single drop of rain that God has not ordained. Every drop was created at an appointed time and sent to carry out a unique purpose. The power of this reality can be further seen and appreciated in the parallel between physical rain and the rain of God's word in your life.

God does not waste his words. There is a unique purpose for every word He allows to land on the ground of your heart. Whether you are aware of it or not, God is always speaking and there is a unique word He has for your current situation. A critical test of spiritual growth and development is seen in your ability to receive His word when it is desirable as well as when it is objectionable. It is often easier to receive what the word has for you, than what the word requires of you.

Yes, it's easy to welcome a word of healing when you are sick, or a word of deliverance when you are bound; a word of prosperity when you are in lack, or a word of encouragement when you are in despair. However, it is a fundamental deception to think that abandoning the requirements of the word, will ultimately yield the blessings of that same word in your life.

God's requirements and blessings go hand in hand. God is always at work in your life creating a better version of you. It is important to develop a spirit of submission that yields to the rain of God's blessings as well as the requirements of God's word.

Lord, help me to maintain a heart of submission in response to anything you allow in my life.

Submission - The Meaning

Submission is the yielding of one's will to the will of another. For the believer, submission is motivated by your obedience to God. It is required in both your relationship with Him and interactions with others.

Submission is an act of humility and is one of the greatest displays of strength. For it forces you to exchange your strength for His. The weaker you are, by laying down your strength, the stronger you can become by taking up His. Submission enables you to carry out His purpose in His strength.

Mirror Moment

When is submission a display of weakness, and when is it an act of obedience?

Submission - The Calling

For they being ignorant of God's righteousness, and going about to establish their own righteousness, have not submitted themselves unto the righteousness of God.   *Romans 10:3*

Submission is the call to conquer the self-righteous enemy within. Righteousness both originates from and is sustained by God alone. The extent to which you share in the righteousness of God is determined by your submission to his will and his way.

Through his life, Jesus demonstrated that righteousness places more emphasis on what a person does than who a person is. Your works will always reveal more about who you are than your words. Submission is the calling to allow your works to testify of your righteousness.

Mirror Moment
What do my actions communicate about my submission to the Lord?

Submission - The Challenges

The challenges associated with submission are often rooted in the fears of insignificance and incompetence. It's amazing how early these fears begin to surface. Even a toddler feels the need to prove that, "I can do it by myself!"

Significance and competence do not replace the need for development. Submission to God and to others is not an assault on your character. Rather, it is an act of character development. It is not intended to break you. It is intended to bless you.

This understanding originated in the garden of Eden, where the blessing was tied to the submission of obedience.[1] Had they continued to walk in that submission, it stands to imagine just how much more God had in store for them.

Mirror Moment
Is my lack of submission to the Lord limiting what he has for my life?

Submission - The Process

The process of submission begins with the understanding that it is ordained by God. Anything that God has ordained for you will producing something good in your life. God only requires of you that which is reasonable or necessary. Yet both are determined by his purpose and not your preference.

Pray for discernment to recognize when others are using your submission for abuse or manipulation. If you find yourself in a situation where your submission is being taken advantage of, pray for the wisdom to determine if endurance, retaliation, or retreat should be your response.

By making himself a prisoner of God,[2] Paul chained himself to God's purpose for his life. He prevented himself from operating independent of that purpose regardless of what it required of him. God always has a larger purpose at play that is beyond your current struggle. You are a steward of the purpose of God for your life and that should take priority over anything that threatens your submission to His will.

Mirror Moment
How should I respond when people take my kindness for granted?

Submission - The Results

Submission keeps you in the most optimal place to see and respond to God's purpose. It causes your goals and ambitions to remain malleable enough to be shaped by God. Submission makes way for the light of God's glory to shine through your life and blind any adversary that would dare oppose it. Your submission is a prerequisite of the elevation that God has in store for your life.[3]

Mirror Moment
Am I allowing my goals and ambitions to be shaped by God?

Assume the Position
The Milestone of Victory

For I am persuaded, that neither death, nor life, nor angels, nor principalities, nor powers, nor things present, nor things to come, Nor height, nor depth, nor any other creature, shall be able to separate us from the love of God, which is in Christ Jesus our Lord.   *Romans 8:38-39*

Your victory is not in your efforts as much as it is in your environment.

My Daily Life Coach

Have you ever found yourself under attack; that for some reason, you had been singled out and left in isolation for a special, ongoing, onslaught of impossible circumstances? Isn't it interesting how trouble has a way of finding your address; and the audacity to walk right in and make itself comfortable in the middle of your discomfort; turning your world upside down and shaking out of your pockets seemingly everything and everyone that contributes to the value, meaning, and quality of your life? How can I walk in victory while in the midst of defeat?

How do I find stability in unstable conditions and security in matters that are outside of my control? Would you believe that the answer is so unbelievably simple that it can be found in just one word: position?

It is by no mistake that both the opening and closing verses of this chapter contain the phrase, in Christ Jesus. The opening verse announces your victory over the internal conflict of such enemies as guilt, failure, and fear discussed in the previous chapter. It then closes with a pronouncement of your victory over everything that could oppose you from the outside.

Your victory is not in your efforts as much as it is in your environment. Your victory is not arbitrary or automatic; it is completely contingent on your position. As deliberate as the author is in echoing the significance of this position in both the first and the last verse of this chapter, you too must be deliberate from the beginning and all throughout your day in reminding yourself, through your words and your witness, of the security and assurance that you have in Christ Jesus.

Lord, help me to stand in the victory that I have in Christ Jesus.

Victory - The Meaning

Victorious living is living life in such a position that the significance of your wins outweighs that of your losses. Two teams can meet in the championship game such that one team may have more losses than its opponent. However, the significance of the championship game is such that if the team with more losses wins, that team is still declared the champion. When you are properly positioned in relationship with Christ, your spiritual and eternal wins exceed any material or relational losses you could ever experience.

Mirror Moment
How am I strengthening my relationship with the Lord?

Victory - The Calling

For everyone born of God overcomes the world. This is the victory that has overcome the world, even our faith.

I John 5:4 NIV

Not only are you called to victorious living, but victory is your inheritance as a child of God. It is not something for which you need to ask. Instead of seeking for it, walk in it; one step at a time. Remember the solidarity of your position is not based upon how you feel. It is based upon what the word has already confirmed.

Mirror Moment
Am I yielding to my feelings or standing in God's truth pertaining to what is presently in front of me?

Victory - The Challenges

The very word victory implies that opposition is at hand. For one party to win, another party has to lose. Depending on the value of what's at stake, neither party is going out without a fight.

Challenges associated with victory fall into the categories of pain and time. The fact that the victory belongs to you, does not mean that it will come in the absence of bruises [just ask Jesus]. Nor does it provide any indication of how long the struggle for that victory will last.

It deepens the satisfaction of your relationship with God when you recognize that He hasn't abandoned you in the difficult seasons of life. He is always there;[1] not as a spectator, but to participate in the struggle even if that means carrying you for part of the way.

Mirror Moment
What am I learning through the challenges that I am presently facing?

Victory - The Process

Living a victorious lifestyle can only be achieved from the inside out. You must begin with your heart not with your hands. You must shift from the posture of doing to the posture of surrendering.

Not only must Christ reside in your heart, but He must also reign there. He must sit on the throne; having jurisdiction over anything that should be there and removing everything that should not.

This won't happen overnight, but it begins with a recognition of what shouldn't be there and a willingness to let it go. In doing so, it releases the fragrance of surrender to God who, in turn, fortifies your position of victory.

Mirror Moment
Am I recognizing and releasing everything in my heart that is not pleasing to God?

Victory - The Results

When you realize that victory already belongs to you, it changes your language, your attitude, and your approach in any situation. You can walk into the office, the classroom, the boardroom, or your very house in full assurance that the God in you is a bigger threat to anything that dares to threaten you there. Victorious living is infectious and attractive. It draws onlookers toward the victor in order to learn how they too can experience victory in their lives.

Mirror Moment
Does my life release a quality that attracts people to God?

Change Your Arsenal
The Milestone of Warfare

Finally, my brethren, be strong in the Lord, and in the power of his might.   *Ephesians 6:10*

As a child of God, you have been equipped with everything that is needed to ensure your success.

My Daily Life Coach

What do you do when you come to the end of yourself; when you encounter a decision, an event, or a season that reveals the limitations of self-reliance? Nothing that you reach for brings the solution that you so desperately desire any closer.

It's frustrating because you are used to eventually figuring it out or waiting it out. However, for some reason, this time is different. You know there's more on the other side of this, but instead of moving forward, you find yourself wastefully marking time; expending energy but going nowhere. The complexity of this recurring reality is simplified in the above passage.

As it relates to standing strong, coming out, and moving forward the answer is always in your arsenal. As a child of God, you have been equipped with everything that is needed to ensure your success. The question becomes, "What are you reaching for?" There is a very popular phrase that speaks of the pointlessness of bringing a knife to a gun fight, and it is along these lines that the author is speaking to his audience.

Victory and progression is found in realizing that any opposition you encounter is deeper than the skin it's in. Defeating this opposition is not accomplished through personal efforts but rather through Divine authority. As a child of God, you have direct access to this authority. However, access is not the same as application. Access implies choice; you can choose to rely on your access or on your own efforts.

As you continue to read through the opening passage, it reveals what you have access to in the arsenal of Divine authority: truth, peace, salvation, faith, and the word of God. This armor is custom designed for the uniqueness of your character and gift mix. It's always a perfect fit and always causes you to experience triumph beyond your imagination.

Lord, help me to both recognize and utilize all that you have provided for me to succeed.

Warfare - The Meaning

Warfare is active engagement in that which pertains to war or conflict. This engagement does not always require fighting, but it does require showing up.

Effective warfare is less about the skill, and more about the heart of the warrior. Less skillful warriors have championed conflicts based on the relentlessness of their resolve.

The value of warfare is optimized when the strength of the opposition has been clearly identified. Breaking the limb of a tree is far less effective than destroying its root.

Mirror Moment
How can I more effectively face the challenges in my life?

Warfare - The Calling

(For the weapons of our warfare are not carnal, but mighty through God to the pulling down of strong holds;) Casting down imaginations, and every high thing that exalteth itself against the knowledge of God, and bringing into captivity every thought to the obedience of Christ;   *2 Corinthians 10:4-5*

For the child of God, warfare is not an option, it is a calling. You have been enlisted into the kingdom of God for such a time as this. It is critical that you proceed with the recognition that your opposition is not skin deep.

The real threat does not meet the eye. He uses this fact to convince you that he is not real, and nothing more than a figment of your imagination. You identify him not by his physical image, but rather by his spiritual agenda.

You are called to stand against any imagination or agenda that is contrary to that of God. Resist the temptation to be passive in response to anything that actively threatens the expansion of God's kingdom in the earth.

Mirror Moment
Do my actions display an active or passive response to anything that threatens God's agenda in my sphere of influence?

145

Warfare - The Challenges

From that time many of his disciples went back, and walked no more with him. Then said Jesus unto the twelve, Will ye also go away?

John 6:66-67

The fear of loneliness is a challenge to contend with when engaging in warfare. It is not easy to take a stand against something when those around you can't see what you see and are more willing to abandon you than to stand with you.

"What's the harm in it?" "Live and let live." "If it ain't broke, don't fix it." These are common sentiments that flow from passively engaged individuals. God does not bring disorder to your attention for you to respond passively to it.

Ask God for wisdom and boldness to respond appropriately to any disorder in your sphere of influence. Stand on the side of the kingdom of God, even if it means standing alone.

Mirror Moment
Does the fear of loneliness and isolation challenge my ability to stand up and speak out for what is right?

Warfare - The Process

Thy kingdom come, Thy will be done in earth, as it is in heaven.
Matthew 6:10

Notice Jesus instruction here is not "rescue us from this earth." Instead, it is let your kingdom come and your will be done in this earth. The coming of his kingdom requires the engagement of his kingdom citizens. Yes, that is you.

This prayer is not to be prayed from the vantage point of a team fan, but rather from that of a team player on a team where Jesus is the captain. The captain rallies and inspires the team as well as communicates the strategy for victory. God is always speaking, even when you cannot hear him.

The first step to effective warfare is to hear from God. His instruction is both general (through his written word) or specific (to your spirit). Identify in the word, that which pertains to the opposition you are facing or sensing. Take that word to God in prayer and ask Him for clarity concerning how you should apply it to the situation at hand. Bring paper and something with which to write. Ask God to confirm what you received and then go and apply it.

Mirror Moment
How would I describe a time when God provided an effective strategy to address a challenge that I was facing?

Warfare - The Results

Effective warfare allows you to remain above, rather than under, the circumstances of your environment. In doing so, you can plant the flag and raise the banner of God's kingdom wherever you are and in whatever you have to face.

Warfare helps you to effectively manage your distractions and remain focused on the tasks at hand. This also yields freedom to those in the same environment who are impacted by the presence of sickness, violence, and confusion.

Remember, you are not only fighting for yourself, but also for the victory of others. Every victory you experience, earns you a badge of confidence and increases your ability for the next encounter.

Mirror Moment
How has my confidence in God been impacted by the victories in my life?

References

Introduction to Daily Life Coach "Can You Hear the Whistle?"
1 St. John 14:16 KJV
2 Matthew 3:16 KJV

Introduction to Volume One Calling
1 Matthew 25:21 KJV
2 Philippians 3:14 KJV
3 II Timothy 1:9 KJV
4 Derek Prince, Set Apart for God: The Beautiful Secret of Holiness
5 Philippians 1:6 KJV

Bible Study
1 II Corinthians 5:7 KJV
2 Romans 10:17 KJV
3 Psalm 46:1 KJV
4 Psalm 1:2 KJV

Communion
1 Ephesians 2:7 KJV

References (cont.)

Declaration
1 Acts 2:1-4 KJV
2 Proverbs 18:21 KJV
3 Matthew 6:9-10 KJV
4 Genesis 2:7 KJV
5 Genesis 6-7 KJV
6 Psalm 19:1 KJV
7 Matthew 17:20 KJV

Evangelism
1 II Corinthians 12:9 KJV
2 Luke 14:23 KJV
3 Psalm 23:5 KJV

Freedom
1 Matthew 11:28 KJV

Inspiration
1 John 4:14 KJV

Investigation
1 I Corinthians 14:33 KJV
2 Hebrews 11:6 KJV

References (cont.)

Prophecy
1 John 19:10-11 KJV
1 Peter 3:15 KJV

Purpose
1 Acts 9:3-5 KJV

Stewardship
1 Psalm 23:3 KJV
2 Proverbs 3:9 KJV

Submission
1 Genesis 3 KJV
2 Ephesians 3:1 KJV
3 James 4:10 KJV

Victory
1 Hebrews 13:5 KJV

Thanks for reading!
Please add a short review on
Amazon and let us know what
you thought!

Connect with us on social media

@allrizemedia

CREATING A LEGACY OF INSPIRATION

ALLRIZE MEDIA

www.allrizemedia.com

Add these to your library today!

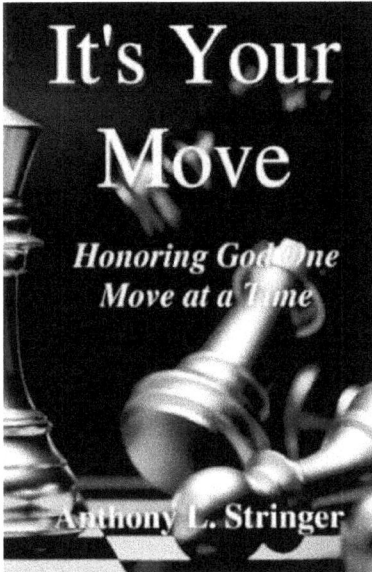

Devotional Journal for Men

Make strategic and purposeful moves that will honor God.

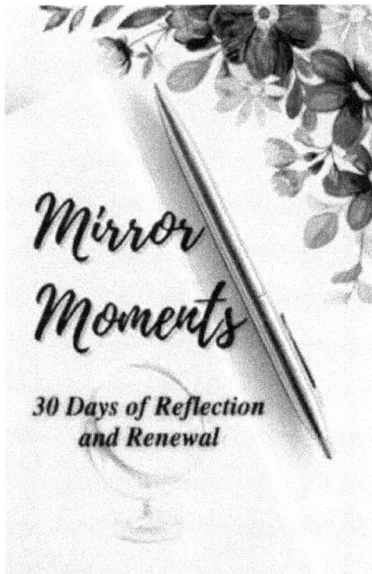

Devotional Journal for Women

See your reflection in the healing streams of God's word.

www.ingramcontent.com/pod-product-compliance
Lightning Source LLC
Chambersburg PA
CBHW060757050426
42449CB00008B/1431